LOW-SALT
COOKERY
100 Healthy & Delicious Main Dishes

LOW-SALT
COOKERY
100 Healthy & Delicious Main Dishes

Contents

ANOTHER BEST-SELLING VOLUME FROM HPBooks®
Publisher: Rick Bailey; Executive Editor: Randy Summerlin
Editorial Director: Elaine R. Woodard; Editor: Jeanette P. Egan
Art Director: Don Burton; Book Design & Assembly: Leslie Sinclair
Production Coordinator: Cindy Coatsworth; Typography: Michelle Carter
Director of Manufacturing: Anthony B. Narducci

Published by HPBooks
A Division of HPBooks, Inc.
P.O. Box 5367, Tucson, AZ 85703   (602) 888-2150
ISBN 0-89586-246-8
Library of Congress Catalog Card Number 86-80777
©1986 HPBooks, Inc.   Printed in the U.S.A.
1st Printing

Originally published as Cooking with Herbs & Spices
©1983 Hennerwood Publications Limited

Cover Photo: Dilled Veal, page 60

Introduction

HOW TO SHAKE THE SALT HABIT

- Use fewer processed foods. They're the major source of hidden salt or sodium.
- Remove the salt shaker from the table. Always taste food before adding salt.
- Read labels. In addition to salt, other words to look for are: Monosodium glutamate, sodium citrate, sodium saccharin, sodium bicarbonate and sodium nitrate. The key word is *sodium*.
- Use fresh or frozen vegetables instead of canned vegetables. With the exception of green peas and lima beans, most plain frozen vegetables do not have added salt.
- Use unsalted butter or margarine for cooking and spreading. These keep best in the freezer; take out as needed.
- Use other seasoning agents, such as herbs, spices, hot-pepper sauce, garlic, onions, wine, fruit juices and vinegar. For cooking, use the same wines that you drink. Cooking wine contains salt.
- Experiment with new flavors. Sometimes a squeeze of lemon juice is all that is needed to go from bland to delicious.
- Make a mixture of your favorite herbs. Keep these in a jar with a shaker top to use in salads or other dishes.
- If possible, gradually reduce the amount of salt used in cooking. You will become accustomed to the taste and you'll notice the flavor of the food instead.
- Use a salt substitute only if recommended by your doctor. The flavor of salt substitutes is not the same as regular salt so you have to become familiar with the new taste.
- Make your own stocks and broths rather than using commercially prepared ones.
- Look for special products with reduced amounts of sodium, such as unsalted canned vegetables or reduced-sodium soy sauce.
- Regular cheeses, canned and processed meats are high in sodium. Look for reduced-sodium alternatives.
- Avoid salted snack items, such as salted potato chips, pretzels and salted popcorn.

SPECIAL PRODUCTS WITH LESS SALT

The following items are only some of the products available with less salt and sodium. Manufacturers have responded to consumer demand for products with decreased amounts of salt. Lower salt items may be in a special section of the supermarket or stocked with similar items. For example, low-salt soups may be with regular soups. Be sure to read the label!

Check your local supermarket for new products. If your supermarket does not have lower salt items available, ask the manager about stocking them.

Unsalted:
Peanut butter
Potato chips
Canned vegetables, such as green beans, whole-kernel corn and canned tomatoes
Cereals
Most plain frozen vegetables, except green peas and lima beans. Frozen vegetables without added salt are a standard item rather than a special one.

Low-Sodium or Reduced-Sodium Products
Butter and margarine
Breads
Soups
Ketchup
Soy sauce
Beef- and chicken-bouillon granules or cubes

SODIUM CONTENT OF RECIPES

Sodium content has been calculated for all recipes in this book using standard tables and a computer nutrient database. Because there are variations between different brands and in foods themselves, the values are approximate. If there is a range of servings for the recipe, sodium content was calculated using the first number of servings listed. Optional items are not included in the sodium calculation.

Salt can be added to any recipe, if desired. However, remember that 1 teaspoon of salt has almost 2000 mg of sodium! These recipes use herbs, spices and other seasoning agents to add flavor without the use of salt.

What's in a Label

According to rules that were passed by the Food and Drug Administration (FDA) in 1984, the following food labels apply to salt and sodium.

No sodium or sodium free: Less than 5 mg sodium per serving.
Very low sodium: 35 mg sodium or less per serving.
Low sodium: 140 mg sodium or less per serving.
Reduced sodium: Sodium content reduced by 75 percent as compared with similar product prepared with salt.
Unsalted: Food product that is normally salted that has been processed without salt, such as *unsalted* whole-kernel corn.

HERBS

For centuries a myriad of herbs have been used in medicine, food and in witchcraft. In medieval times no king, lord or abbot would be without his herb garden. These herbs were not grown for their beauty, but they were used in cooking to mask the flavor of aging meat and scattered liberally in homes to sweeten the atmosphere.

In recent years the demand for natural products has led to a revival of interest in herbs. Also, as more and more health authorities have recommended a reduction in salt intake, more people are turning to herbs and spices as flavoring agents. The introduction of ethnic cuisines has also done much to spark an interest in the use of herbs, spices and exotic seasonings.

Use fresh herbs generously; because dried herbs are more concentrated, use them more moderately. Substitute one-third to one-half the amount of dried herbs for fresh herbs.

Individual Herbs

Bay leaf—the leaves are an indispensable part of a bouquet garni. This pungent herb is used in dishes, such as stews or spaghetti sauces, that cook for awhile. The California bay is stronger than the European bay laurel.

Basil—its evocative, rather clove-like smell spells out Mediterranean sunshine. Use fresh basil if possible. Basil is used in Italian cuisine; it goes well with tomatoes and other vegetables.

Caraway—the seeds have a distinctive flavor as everyone who has eaten a real goulash knows. Caraway seeds are used in cakes, cookies, rye bread and cabbage.

Chervil—beloved of the French and an essential ingredient in *omelette fines herbes*. In fact, it complements parsley and tarragon to perfection, bringing out their flavors. It has a slight-anise flavor.

Chives—have a delicate onion flavor and are used for both their flavor and as a garnish.

Cilantro—the plant that produces coriander seed. When the leaves are used fresh, they are called cilantro. Cilantro is used extensively in Mexican and Chinese food. It is used in salsa, guacamole, soups and stews. It's especially good with shrimp.

Dill—unbeatable as a garnish for fish. When fresh dill is not available, substitute *dill weed* not dill seed. Dill weed is the herb used in pickled cucumbers. Fresh dill loses its delicate flavor in cooking, so it is best added just before serving. Dill is also used in bread and vegetables, such as carrots, green beans and potatoes.

Fennel—fresh, feathery fennel looks similar to dill, but fennel has a strong anise flavor. Fennel goes well in pasta, salads and breads. The bulb is delicious when finely chopped and added to a tomato or fish salad.

Ginger—fresh gingerroot is widely available. Peel or scrape, then grate or finely chop before using. Some recipes suggest bruising the gingerroot. Bruise by placing gingerroot piece on a flat surface; hit with a heavy object, such as a rolling pin. This helps release the juices during cooking; remove bruised gingerroot before serving if desired.

Dried gingerroot is available as ground ginger. Crystallized or candied ginger and stem ginger in syrup are also available.

Garlic—the whole garlic is a bulb and each section is a clove. Many dishes, such as pesto or garlic bread, would not be the same without this pungent flavoring. Garlic cloves are usually peeled, then mashed or finely chopped before using. A garlic press can be used, but it is not a necessity.

Horseradish—a root rather like a parsnip but with a strong flavor and smell. Horseradish can be grated and stored in the refrigerator. Mix with sour cream or whipped cream for a sauce. It can be bought already prepared. Dried powdered horseradish is also available. Horseradish goes well with roast beef and fish. It's an essential component of red cocktail sauce for seafood.

Juniper berries—have a rather sweet pine-like flavor. The berries are usually crushed before using to release the full flavor. They can be tied in a cheesecloth bag if you want to remove them before serving. They are used in marinades for game.

1. Bay leaves
2. Caraway seeds
3. Chives
4. Chervil
5. Cilantro
6. Dill
7. Fennel
8. Gingerroot
9. Garlic clove
10. Juniper berries
11. Lemongrass
12. Parsley
13. Mint
14. Oregano
15. Sage
16. Tarragon
17. Rosemary
18. Savory
19. Sorrel
20. Thyme

Lemongrass (serai)—clumps of this grass grow in tropical climates. It is used extensively in Southeast Asia. The stems, which look like a miniature leek, are sold in some supermarkets and Chinese shops in bundles of three or four stems. Lemongrass can be stored in the refrigerator 2 to 3 weeks or frozen. To use lemongrass, cut off root end, then thinly slice, bruise or process in a blender or food processor fitted with the steel blade until pureed. It's easy to freeze the puree. Pack into small airtight containers; label with the number of stems because most recipes call for a certain number of stems. Dried powdered lemongrass, usually called *serai* or *sereh*, is also available. Buy it in small quantities. Strips of lemon peel are the best substitute, but use the real thing if it's available. Lemongrass is used to flavor curries, soups, sauces and fish dishes.

Marjoram and oregano—both members of the oregano family, marjoram is sweeter with a flower-like perfume. It is one of the most useful and popular herbs and can be grown in a pot in the kitchen throughout the winter. It loses its delicate flavor quickly in cooking, so it is best added just before serving. Marjoram and oregano are used extensively in Italian cooking.

Mint—this family has many members. Perhaps two of the best known are peppermint and spearmint. Mint is used in many Middle Eastern dishes, such as tabbouleh and lamb. Mint is excellent in sorbets and beverages, such as minted iced tea.

Parsley—the universal garnish, parsley is best used fresh in liberal quantities. This is another family with many members. Curly parsley is the one most often used for garnishing, but flat-leafed parsley or Italian parsley often is preferred for cooking. Parsley is used in herbed butters and butter sauces. It is sometimes deep fried, then used as a garnish in Chinese cooking.

Rosemary—known as the herb of remembrance, love and friendship. Try to grow a bush near the kitchen door. Place bruised sprigs under lamb roasts or fish before cooking. Use sparingly as the flavor can be overpowering. Rosemary is an evergreen, so it is available throughout the year. It flourishes in a well-drained, sunny spot. Rosemary is used in both sweet and savory dishes. It is sometimes added to jams or jellies.

Sage—fresh sage has a strong, pronounced flavor. Dried sage is not as pungent, but it is still full of flavor. Use with discretion. Sage goes well in rich foods, such as pork, goose, duck, sausages, liver and cheese. Much of the aroma of Thanksgiving dinner is due to the use of sage in the stuffing for the turkey.

Savory—winter savory is stronger in flavor than the summer variety. Both have a peppery flavor. Summer savory is an annual, and winter savory is a perennial. Savory gives a lift to salads and is particularly good when sprinkled over buttered new peas or green beans.

Sorrel—large tart leaves. Sorrel can be torn into pieces and used raw in salads. Or cook as for spinach and puree for sauces to serve with fish, veal or egg dishes. It can also be used in soups. It is used in the traditional green mayonnaise, *sauce vert*, served with baked or poached salmon or salmon trout.

Tarragon—one of the great herbs. It will transform ordinary chicken into something special. Tarragon complements fish and egg dishes, looks pretty as a garnish and makes a delicious herb butter to serve with grilled veal, fish or chicken. It's a delicious addition to a mayonnaise dressing for fish, too. Tarragon is the main flavoring ingredient in béarnaise sauce, and it is also used to flavor vinegar.

Thyme—is highly aromatic. It blends well with a variety of other herbs in sauces, stuffings and dumplings. Lemon thyme has a more delicate flavor and therefore complements chicken, veal and fish dishes.

Bouquet Garni

Cut a 3-inch cheesecloth square. Place 2 bay leaves, 2 or 3 sprigs each of parsley and thyme or marjoram, 6 peppercorns and 1 garlic clove, if desired, on cheesecloth. Bring edge of cheesecloth up to form a bag. Tie securely with kitchen string.

SPICES

For centuries travellers, explorers and pioneers risked life and limb to bring spices first to Arabia, then to the Mediterranean and the markets of Europe. The Arabs held onto this trade for almost 1000 years. The Romans then monopolized the trade after discovering they could boat across to India following the monsoons. For centuries the trade between the East and Europe continued, then in the 1490s the race began to control India and the Spice Islands of the East.

In 1498, Portuguese explorers sailed eastwards and commandeered the spice trade from the Arabs. The Dutch took the trade in 1605, and by 1796 Britain had taken over almost all the Dutch interests. The cultivation of spices became more widespread, the price dropped and now we can enjoy spices from all over the world.

Individual Spices

Allspice—so-called because it has a hint of cloves, nutmeg and cinnamon, although it is, in fact, a single spice. It is available powdered and as dried whole berries.

Cardamom—small, triangular-shaped pods which contain tiny brownish-black seeds. To remove these, use a pestle and mortar to crack the pod or squeeze it between your finger and thumb. It gives a warm, pungent flavor to foods. In some dishes the pods are bruised or cracked but left whole.

Cayenne—not to be confused with paprika, though they are all members of the large capsicum pepper family. Cayenne is a hot and pungent powder.

Chili powder—a powerful blend of several species of small red chilies. Buy it in small quantities and use judiciously. Some chili-powder blends may contain salt.

Whole chilies—finger-shaped red peppers can be bought fresh or dried. Treat these with great respect, especially the fresh variety. Wear rubber gloves when preparing fresh chilies. Do not touch your eyes after handling them. Chili peppers vary in hotness. Start with a lesser amount, then add more to taste as needed. The seeds are especially pungent. Chop the flesh finely in a blender or food processor or pound in a pestle and mortar before using in curries or sweet and sour dishes. *Dried chilies* are left whole when used for pickling.

Cinnamon—spicy, sweet and fragrant. Thin shavings of bark are rolled into quills or cigar shapes and dried; the not-so-perfect shapes are ground for use in baking.

Cloves—give a rich, warm aroma. Cloves are flower buds from a tree. Cloves are available whole and ground. They are an important ingredient in curries, but use with dis-

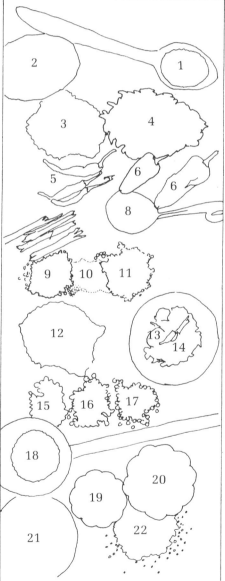

1. Ground red (cayenne) pepper
2. Allspice berries
3. Ground chilies
4. Cardamon pods
5. Dried chilies
6. Fresh chilies
7. Cinnamon sticks or quills
8. Whole cloves
9. Fenugreek
10. Mustard seeds
11. Coriander seeds
12. Paprika
13. Whole nutmeg
14. Mace blades
15. Black peppercorns
16. Green peppercorns
17. White peppercorns
18. Poppy seeds
19. Saffron
20. Turmeric
21. Dried tamarind
22. Sesame seeds

cretion because the flavor can become overpowering. Ground cloves are used a great deal in baking.

Coriander—tiny round seeds which, when dry-fried and crushed, give off a burnt orange-peel fragrance. It is one of the principal ingredients in curry powder. Fresh coriander leaves are called cilantro.

Cumin—a pungent-flavored seed which looks similar to but is much smaller than fennel. It is essential in curry powders and is used extensively in North African and Mexican dishes.

Fenugreek—an ingredient of nearly all curry powders. The seeds are yellowish-brown. Dry-fry before grinding to bring out the flavor. It is not recommended for use with recipes other than for curried fish or meat.

Mustard seed—black and brown seeds used in curry powders. They are also used in pickling spice and in such pickles as piccalilli.

Nutmeg and mace—the nutmeg is the inner kernel of the nutmeg fruit. When ripe the fruit splits open like a chestnut revealing bright red arils; these are the mace which surround the nutmeg. The color of the mace, when exposed to the air, becomes a deep-orange color. When the mace is removed, the shell of the nut is cracked to remove the nutmeg. These pieces of mace are described as blades and have a similar but more delicate flavor than nutmeg. Nutmeg is available whole or ground. Mace is available as blades or ground.

Paprika—mild and spicy with a hint of sweetness. It comes in varying shades from red to brown in color. It adds color as well as flavor to foods. Use it liberally.

Peppercorns—pepper is one of the oldest and certainly the world's most important spice. Pepper is available as ground white and black pepper and as green, black or white peppercorns.

Poppy seeds—easily recognized by their slate-blue color and nutlike flavor. They are often scattered like sesame seeds on breads and rolls. Poppy seeds are also used as a filling for coffeecakes.

Saffron—the dried stigmas of the yellow crocus. It is the world's most expensive spice. Saffron is essential for a genuine paella and for Italian risottos. It gives an exquisite flavor but is used in such minute quantities that its main purpose is to give its delicate yellow color to food. To prepare, place a few strands of saffron into a cup. Pour over a little boiling water or stock. Let steep, then use. Turmeric is sometimes used as a substitute, but neither the color nor flavor is as subtle.

Sesame seeds—combine with a wide variety of foods. The seeds are sweet and are especially nutty when toasted. They can be made into sesame-seed paste, an ingredient used in Middle Eastern cooking.

Tamarind—gives an essential tartness to many dishes from Southeast Asia and India. It can be bought in pulp or dried form, the latter looking like slices of dried apple. It is usually soaked before using.

Turmeric—has a rich, warm, disinctive smell and gives a strong yellow color. It comes from the ginger family and is available ground.

OTHER SPECIAL INGREDIENTS

Bouillon granules—very low- and low-sodium bouillon granules are available as well as regular bouillon gran-ules. Use as substitutes for canned or homemade beef and chicken stocks or broths.

Ketchup—tomato product containing sugar, salt and spices. A low-sodium version is available.

Soy sauce—used for seasoning in oriental dishes. If you are cutting back on salt, look for low-sodium soy sauce.

Unsalted tomato sauce—tomato sauce processed without added salt.

Unsalted peanut butter—peanut butter processed without added salt.

SPECIAL TECHNIQUES

Bruising or crushing spices—Spices and seasonings can be crushed in a pestle and mortar, with the flat side of a large knife or with a heavy object, such as a rolling pin. Crushing whole spices allows the flavor to be released into the food more easily.

Dry-frying coconut—put unsweetened shredded coconut into a wok or a large skillet over medium heat. Heat, stirring constantly, until the coconut is dry, crisp and golden brown. Do not be tempted to leave it, or it will burn. Process in a blender or food processor until the coconut becomes an oily paste. This acts as a thickening agent as well as adding color and flavor.

Dry-frying spices—heat a heavy skillet over low heat. Add whole spices. Heat, stirring, until spices give off a spicy aroma, 2 to 3 minutes. Remove, cool and grind.

Grinding spices—in addition to the familiar pepper grinder, there are also nutmeg grinders and nutmeg graters. Special spice grinders are available for grinding whole spices. Spices can also be ground in a blender or with a *mortar and pestle*.

Roasting peanuts—preheat oven to 400F (205C). Place shelled peanuts in a baking pan. Roast about 10 minutes, shaking the tray once or twice during roasting so nuts roast evenly. Pour out on a clean, dry towel. Fold up into a bundle; rub vigorously to remove skins.

Zesting citrus fruit—citrus zest can be removed by shredding or with a small knife or citrus zester. Use only the colored part of the peel; discard the bitter white layer.

Fish & Seafood

Grilled Fish Steaks

4 (6-oz.) firm-textured fish steaks, such as tuna
1/4 cup vegetable oil
Freshly ground pepper
1 teaspoon dried leaf tarragon
1 teaspoon low-sodium soy sauce
1 tablespoon lemon juice

1. Preheat grill; place grill rack 4 inches from coals. Rinse fish; pat dry with paper towels. Place fish in a shallow baking pan. In a small bowl, combine oil, pepper, tarragon, soy sauce and lemon juice.
2. Pour oil mixture over fish. Cover and let marinate while coals heat, about 30 minutes.
3. Place marinated fish on rack over hot coals, reserving marinade. Brush fish with marinade and turn while grilling. Grill until fish turns from transparent to opaque, about 5 to 6 minutes. Makes 4 servings.

About 115 mg sodium per serving.

Salmon-Stuffed Tomatoes

4 large tomatoes
2 tablespoons unsalted butter or margarine
1 small onion, chopped
1/2 lb. salmon, cooked, flaked
1-1/2 cups fresh reduced-sodium-bread crumbs
1 egg, beaten
1 teaspoon dried leaf tarragon
Freshly ground pepper

1. Preheat oven to 350F (175C). Grease a baking dish.
2. Cut a thin slice from top of each tomato. Scoop out pulp; reserve pulp, discarding seeds.
3. Melt butter or margarine in a medium saucepan. Add onion; sauté until soft, 5 minutes. Remove from heat; stir in reserved tomato pulp, salmon, bread crumbs, egg, pepper and tarragon.
4. Spoon mixture into prepared tomatoes. Place stuffed tomatoes in greased baking dish.
5. Bake in preheated oven until heated through, about 20 minutes. Serve hot. Makes 4 servings.

About 60 mg sodium per serving.

Grilled Fish Steaks

Dilled Fish Salad

1 lb. halibut or other fish, cooked, flaked
1/2 large cucumber, peeled, coarsely chopped
1 small onion, chopped
1 celery stalk, chopped
1/2 cup Mustard & Dill Mayonnaise, page 77
1/2 cup dairy sour cream
Freshly ground pepper

To garnish:
4 tomatoes, quartered
2 tablespoons chopped fresh chives

1. In a medium bowl, combine fish, cucumber, onion and celery.
2. In a small bowl, combine mayonnaise, sour cream and pepper. Stir mayonnaise mixture into fish mixture. Cover salad and refrigerate until chilled, 2 to 3 hours.
3. To serve, arrange salad in a serving bowl. Arrange tomatoes around edge of bowl. Sprinkle with chives. Makes 4 servings.

About 120 mg sodium per serving.

Poached Salmon with Herbs

Poached Salmon with Herbs

2 cups water
1 cup dry white wine
1 bay leaf
5 lemon slices
3 or 4 tarragon sprigs
1 teaspoon peppercorns
6 (5-oz.) salmon steaks
1 recipe Watercress Mayonnaise, page 76

To garnish:
Watercress

1. In a large skillet, combine water, wine, bay leaf, lemon slices, tarragon and peppercorns. Bring to a boil over high heat.
2. Add salmon to boiling liquid. Reduce heat to low. Cover and simmer until salmon turns from transparent to opaque, 8 to 10 minutes. Remove fish from poaching liquid with a slotted spatula.
3. Serve warm or cover and refrigerate until chilled. Garnish with watercress. Serve with Watercress Mayonnaise. Makes 6 servings.

About 80 mg sodium per serving.

Sautéed Fish Fillets

4 (4- to 5-oz.) fish fillets
1 recipe Simple Marinade, page 78
1/2 cup all-purpose flour
2 tablespoons unsalted butter or margarine
3 tablespoons vegetable oil

1. Place fillets in a shallow dish. Pour marinade over fillets; cover and marinate 1 to 2 hours.
2. Remove with tongs. Dip into flour to coat.
3. Heat butter and oil in a large skillet. Add floured fillets; sauté until until browned and fish turns from transparent to opaque, 8 to 10 minutes, turning once. Makes 4 servings.

About 85 mg sodium per serving.

Salmon Seviche

1-1/2 lbs. fresh salmon or other firm-textured fish
3/4 cup dry white wine
1/3 cup walnut oil or olive oil
1 small onion, sliced
1 garlic clove, crushed
Juice of 1/2 orange
Juice of 1 lemon
White pepper

To garnish:
2 teaspoons chopped chives

1. Remove skin and any bones from fish. Cut into small strips; place in a shallow dish.
2. In a small bowl, combine wine, oil, onion, garlic, orange juice, lemon juice and pepper. Pour over fish. Cover and refrigerate about 8 hours, stirring occasionally.
3. Drain fish, discarding marinade. Spoon into a serving bowl. Sprinkle with chopped chives. Makes 8 appetizers.

Variation
Spoon drained fish into 8 avocado halves. Sprinkle with chopped chives. Serve as a first course.

About 89 mg sodium per serving.
About 95 mg sodium per serving with 1 avocado half.

Fish & Mushroom Salad in Horseradish Sauce

Fish & Mushroom Salad in Horseradish Sauce

1 lb. halibut or other fish, cooked, flaked
1/4 lb. mushrooms, sliced
4 to 6 green onions, chopped
1/2 cup whipping cream
3 tablespoons prepared horseradish
1/2 cup plain yogurt
Freshly ground pepper

To serve:
Lettuce leaves
1/2 teaspoon mustard seeds
Chopped green-onion tops

1. In a medium bowl, combine fish, mushrooms and green onions; set aside.

2. In a small bowl, whip cream until soft peaks form. Stir in horseradish and yogurt. Season with pepper. Pour cream mixture over fish. Stir until combined. Cover and refrigerate until chilled, 2 to 3 hours.
3. To serve, line a serving bowl with lettuce leaves. Spoon salad over lettuce. Sprinkle salad with mustard seeds and chopped onion tops. Makes 4 servings.

About 115 mg sodium per serving.

Fish Kabobs with Coconut Marinade

1-1/2 lbs. firm-textured fish, such as monkfish, halibut or haddock, skinned
1/4 lb. mushrooms
1/2 red bell pepper, cut into squares
1/2 green bell pepper, cut into wide squares
Vegetable oil

Marinade:
2 garlic cloves
1 (1-inch) piece gingerroot, sliced
1 small onion, peeled
3 or 4 cilantro leaves
1/2 teaspoon chili powder
1/2 teaspoon ground turmeric
1 cup Coconut Milk, page 76

To serve:
Lemon wedges

The fish and delicate coconut marinade complement each other well. The red, green and yellow colors are pleasing, too. If you cannot get monkfish, select thick pieces of halibut or haddock, so that the chunky pieces will stay on the skewers during cooking. Use wooden or bamboo skewers. Soak skewers in water while fish is marinating to prevent them from burning during cooking.

1. Soak 20 bamboo skewers in water at least 2 hours. Cut fish into 1-inch cubes; place in a shallow bowl.
2. To make marinade, in a blender or food processor fitted with the steel blade, process garlic, gingerroot, onion and cilantro leaves until pureed. Add chili powder, turmeric and coconut milk.
3. Pour marinade over fish cubes. Cover and refrigerate about 2 hours, stirring occasionally.
4. Place oven rack about 6 inches from heat source. Preheat broiler. Alternately thread marinated fish, mushrooms and bell peppers onto skewers. Brush with a little oil. Broil under preheated broiler until fish turns from transparent to opaque, about 10 minutes, turning frequently.
5. Serve with lemon wedges. Makes 4 servings.

Variation
This dish is also delicious cooked on a barbecue.

About 115 mg sodium per serving.

Trout Pinwheels with Cheese Sauce

1-1/2 lbs. boneless trout fillets, skinned
White pepper
Juice of 1 lemon

Cheese Sauce:
1-1/2 tablespoons unsalted butter or margarine
1-1/2 tablespoons flour
1/2 cup milk
1/2 cup water and 1/2 teaspoon low-sodium chicken-bouillon granules
1 cup shredded reduced-sodium Swiss cheese (4 oz.)
2 teaspoons finely chopped dill or 1/2 teaspoon dill weed
Hot-pepper sauce

1. Preheat oven to 425F (220C). Lightly grease a 13'' x 9'' baking dish. Season fillets with white pepper; sprinkle with lemon juice.
2. Roll up fillets, starting from small end; secure with wooden picks. Place rolled fillets in greased baking dish.
3. Bake in preheated oven until fish tests done, about 10 minutes.
4. Meanwhile make sauce. To make sauce, melt butter or margarine in a medium saucepan. Add flour; cook, stirring, 2 minutes. Slowly stir in milk, water and bouillon granules. Cook, stirring, until sauce is smooth and thickened. Stir in cheese, dill and hot-pepper sauce. Stir until cheese melts.
5. Place fillets on individual plates. Pour pan juices into sauce. Spoon sauce over fillets. Makes 4 servings.

About 135 mg sodium per serving.

Reduced-Sodium Cheeses

Reduced-sodium cheeses are available. For example, reduced-sodium Swiss cheese has only 35 mg sodium per ounce compared to 200 mg sodium for some regular Swiss cheese. Some reduced-sodium cheeses are also lower in fat and cholesterol than regular cheeses.

Trout Pinwheels with Cheese Sauce

Canadian Chowder

1 lb. cod or haddock fillets
3 cups water
2 tablespoons unsalted butter or margarine
1 lb. red-skinned potatoes, peeled, diced
1 medium onion, chopped
1-1/2 cups milk
White pepper
2 tablespoons chopped parsley
2 tablespoons chopped chives

1. Place fish and water in a large saucepan. Bring to a boil. Reduce heat. Cover and simmer 10 minutes. Pour into a strainer, reserving cooking liquid. Cool fish slightly. Remove and discard skin and bones. Flake fish; set aside.
2. Melt butter or margarine in a medium skillet. Add onion; sauté until softened. Return to pan; add potatoes and sautéed onions. Cover and cook until potatoes are just tender, 10 to 15 minutes.
3. Add reserved flaked fish, white pepper, parsley and chives. Bring to a boil; add milk. Heat through; do not boil. Makes 6 servings.

About 135 mg sodium per serving.

Mild Curried Seafood

1/2 lb. scallops, thawed if frozen
1/2 lb. halibut or other fish, cut in 1-inch cubes
3 tablespoons vegetable oil
1 garlic clove, crushed
1 small onion, chopped
1 teaspoon Mild Curry Powder, page 75
1 cup dry white wine
2 bay leaves
1/2 cup water and 1/2 teaspoon low-sodium chicken-bouillon granules
1 tablespoon unsalted butter or margarine blended with 2 tablespoons all-purpose flour
2 cups hot cooked rice, cooked without salt

To garnish:
1/4 teaspoon paprika
Green-onion curls, page 31

1. Dry scallops and halibut on paper towels; set aside.
2. Heat 2 tablespoons oil in a medium skillet over medium heat. Add garlic and onion; sauté until softened. Add curry powder; cook, stirring constantly, 1 to 2 minutes.
3. Add wine, bay leaves, scallops and fish; bring to a boil. Reduce heat. Cover and simmer until scallops and fish turn from transparent to opaque, about 5 minutes. Do not overcook. Remove scallops and fish with a slotted spoon; place in a serving bowl. Keep hot. Discard bay leaves.
4. Add water and bouillon granules to cooking liquid. Add butter mixture in small pieces, stirring. Boil until thickened, stirring constantly. Pour sauce over scallops and fish.
5. In a small bowl, combine paprika and remaining 1 tablespoon oil; pour mixture over surface of dish to garnish.
6. Garnish with green-onion curls. Serve with rice. Makes 4 servings.

About 135 mg sodium per serving.

Piri Piri Shrimp

3/4 to 1 teaspoon chili powder
Juice of 1 lemon
1-1/4 lbs. peeled shrimp, thawed if frozen
Vegetable oil

To garnish:
Lemon wedges
Cilantro leaves

This recipe comes from Mozambique. Shrimp are expensive but are luxurious as an appetizer for a special occasion. Finish the meal with dishes that are low in salt.

1. Combine chili powder and lemon juice in a medium bowl. Stir in shrimp; cover and refrigerate about 1 hour.
2. In a deep saucepan, heat 3 inches oil to 360F (180C) or until a 1-inch bread cube turns golden brown in 60 seconds. Pat shrimp dry with paper towels. Add shrimp to hot oil in batches; cook until pink, 1 to 2 minutes. Do not overcook.
3. Serve very hot. Garnish with lemon wedges and cilantro leaves. Makes 8 appetizer servings.

About 125 mg sodium per serving.

Piri Piri Shrimp

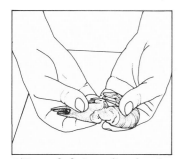
1/To peel shrimp, first break off heads if they are still attached.

2/To remove shell, pull off legs and open the shell lengthwise.

3/To remove intestinal vein, cut down center back; lift out vein.

Cooking Fish

Cook fish until it turns from translucent to opaque or just *begins* to flake. Check for doneness by gently inserting a fork into the center of the thickest part. Once fish flakes, it is overcooked, tough and dry. A general rule is to cook fish 10 minutes per inch of thickness.

Crabs in Chili Sauce

2 live medium crabs, about 1-1/2 lbs. each, cooked without salt
1/4 cup vegetable oil
1 (1-inch) piece gingerroot, chopped
2 to 3 garlic cloves, crushed
1 to 2 fresh red chilies, seeded, finely chopped, or hot-pepper sauce to taste
2/3 cup low-sodium ketchup
2 tablespoons brown sugar
1 teaspoon low-sodium soy sauce
1/2 cup boiling water

In Malaysia and Singapore, these crabs are eaten with the fingers. Have lots of paper napkins and a large bowl for shells. Serve with hot cooked rice or crusty bread and chunky pieces of cucumber.

1. Twist off large claws. Using your thumbs, lift off top shell. Turn crab on its back; lift up and discard apron. Discard bile sac and gray feathery gills.
2. Using a teaspoon, scrape all brown creamy meat (crab butter) from top shell into a small bowl.
3. Twist legs from body. Cut body section in half. Crack large claws and small legs using nutcrackers, a hammer or blunt edge of a cleaver.
4. Heat oil in a large skillet or wok. Add gingerroot, garlic and chilies, if using; sauté 2 minutes.
5. Add ketchup, sugar, soy sauce and hot-pepper sauce, if using.
6. When hot, stir crab pieces, crabmeat and water into sauce; cook over high heat until heated through.
7. Spoon into a serving dish or serve straight from wok. Makes 4 servings.

About 165 mg sodium per serving.

Clockwise from top left: Steamed Fish; Chinese-Style Pork Stew, page 50; Crabs in Chili Sauce

Steamed Fish

1 (1-1/4-lb.) sole or flounder, cleaned, head on
Freshly ground pepper
Vegetable oil
1 (1-inch) piece gingerroot, shredded

Onion Sauce:
2 tablespoons vegetable oil
2 small onions, sliced
1 teaspoon low-sodium soy sauce
1 tablespoon sesame oil

To garnish:
Green-onion curls, see box page 31
Cilantro leaves

Fish steaks or fillets can be substituted for whole fish.

1. Dry fish with paper towels. Using a sharp knife, make 2 slashes in each side of fish; rub with pepper. Line a steamer with foil to retain cooking juices. Place fish on foil. Brush with oil; sprinkle with gingerroot. Cover and steam until fish turns from transparent to opaque, about 25 minutes. Or, bake fish in a greased dish in a preheated 375F (190C) oven about 30 minutes.
2. To make sauce, heat oil in a medium skillet. Add onions; sauté until softened. Pour juices from foil tray or baking dish into skillet. Add soy sauce and sesame oil.
3. Transfer fish to a serving dish; pour sauce over fish. Garnish with green-onion curls and cilantro. Makes 4 servings.

About 130 mg sodium per serving.

Fish Moolie

4-1/4 cups shredded coconut (about 12 oz.)
1-1/2 cups boiling water
1 medium onion
6 whole blanched almonds
2 or 3 garlic cloves
1 (1-inch) piece gingerroot, thinly sliced
2 lemongrass stems
2 to 3 teaspoons ground turmeric
3 tablespoons vegetable oil
1-1/4 lbs. monkfish, halibut or other firm-textured fish fillets, skinned, cut into 1-inch cubes
1 to 3 fresh red chilies, seeded, thinly sliced

To garnish:
Parsley or cilantro sprigs

This is a popular fish curry from Southeast Asia. Choose a firm-textured fish so the pieces remain whole during the brief cooking. Some of the coconut is toasted, then reduced to a paste.

1. Place 1 cup coconut in a heavy medium skillet or wok; heat until dry, golden and crisp, turning constantly to prevent burning. This will take several minutes. In a blender, process toasted coconut until it appears oily. Place coconut into a small bowl; set aside.
2. Make coconut milk with remaining coconut and boiling water as described on page 76. When cream rises to top of coconut milk, spoon off 1/4 cup; set coconut milk and coconut cream aside.
3. In a blender or food processor fitted with a steel blade, process onion, almonds, garlic, gingerroot and 2-1/2 inches from root end of lemongrass stems into a paste. Add turmeric. Reserve remaining lemongrass.
4. Heat oil in a large skillet or wok. Add onion paste; fry, stirring, 3 to 4 minutes. Do not brown. Add coconut milk, stirring constantly to prevent curdling.
5. Add fish, 3/4 of chilies and remaining lemongrass. Reduce heat. Simmer, uncovered, 3 to 4 minutes. Stir in blended coconut; cook until fish turns from transparent to opaque, 2 to 3 minutes.
6. Stir in coconut cream; heat through. Remove lemongrass stems. Spoon into a serving dish; sprinkle with remaining chilies. Garnish with parsley or cilantro. Makes 4 servings.

About 100 mg sodium per serving.

Shrimp Curry

1/3 cup unsalted butter or margarine
1/4 cup all-purpose flour
1 tablespoon Hot Curry Powder, page 75
1 tablespoon finely grated gingerroot
2 cups Coconut Milk, page 76
1/2 cup Unsalted Chicken Stock, page 79, or 1/2 cup
    water and 1/2 teaspoon reduced-sodium
    chicken-bouillon granules
1 tablespoon lemon juice
1-1/2 lbs. peeled shrimp, cooked

To serve:
3 cups hot cooked rice, cooked without salt
Condiments, such as unsalted nuts, shredded coconut,
    bell-pepper strips and raisins

1. Melt butter or margarine in a large saucepan. Stir in flour. Cook, stirring, 2 minutes.
2. Stir in curry powder and gingerroot. Slowly stir in coconut milk, stock and lemon juice. Cook, stirring, until thickened. Stir in shrimp; heat through.
3. Serve with rice and condiments. Makes 6 servings.

About 165 mg sodium per serving.

Sole & Lime Rolls

6 tablespoons unsalted butter or margarine, room
    temperature
2 tablespoons chopped chives
3/4 cup fresh reduced-sodium-bread crumbs
Grated peel of 1 lime
About 1/4 cup lime juice
Freshly ground pepper
8 (4- to 6-oz.) sole fillets, skinned

To garnish:
Lime twists
Chopped chives

1. Preheat broiler. Grease a shallow baking pan large enough to hold rolled fillets in 1 layer.
2. In a small bowl, beat butter or margarine and chives until soft and creamy. Stir in bread crumbs, lime peel and enough lime juice to make a good spreading consistency. Season with pepper.
3. Spread sole fillets with equal amounts of butter mixture. Roll up from small end; secure with wooden picks. Place rolled fillets on edge in greased baking pan.
4. Broil 5 minutes. Turn over with tongs. Broil until fish turns from transparent to opaque, about 5 minutes.
5. Place on individual plates; garnish with lime twists and chives. Serve hot. Makes 4 servings.

About 130 mg sodium per serving.

Shrimp Curry with condiments

South African Pickled Fish

2 lbs. haddock fillets, skinned
3/4 cup all-purpose flour
2 eggs, beaten
Vegetable oil

Curry Sauce:
1-1/2 cups malt vinegar
1 tablespoon Hot or Mild Curry Powder, page 75
1-1/2 teaspoons ground turmeric
1 teaspoon all-purpose flour
3/4 cup water
3 tablespoons brown sugar
8 bay leaves
20 peppercorns
3 or 4 large onions, sliced

To garnish:
1 green bell pepper, cut into strips or rings
1 red bell pepper, cut into strips or rings
1 lemon, sliced
Fresh bay leaves, if desired

This is a marvelous dish for a buffet. It should be cooked at least 2 days ahead and requires very little last-minute attention. It is also a delicious and unusual way of serving up a humble and not so expensive fish. Serve with a rice salad, grated carrots, chutney and shredded coconut.

1. Cut fish into 3" x 2" pieces. Dip fish pieces in flour. Dip into beaten eggs, then back into flour.
2. Heat 3 inches oil in a deep skillet to 360F (180C) or until a 1-inch bread cube turns golden brown in 60 seconds. Add coated fish in batches. Fry until golden brown and fish turns from opaque to transparent, about 4 minutes per side. Drain on paper towels.
3. To make curry sauce, in a medium bowl, combine 1 tablespoon vinegar, curry powder, turmeric and flour; set aside. Combine remaining vinegar, water and sugar in a medium saucepan. Cook over low heat, stirring, until sugar dissolves.
4. Stir flour paste into hot liquid. Add bay leaves and peppercorns. Bring to a boil, stirring constantly. Add onion slices. Cook 5 minutes; cool slightly.
5. Place a layer of fish in a deep casserole. Add some onions from sauce. Repeat in layers until all fish and onions are used up. Pour sauce over top. Cover with a lid or foil. Refrigerate 2 days.
6. To serve, arrange fish and onions in a serving dish. Garnish with bell peppers, lemon slices and fresh bay leaves, if desired. Makes 6 servings.

About 116 mg sodium per serving.

Sweet & Sour Fish

1 (1-1/2- to 2-lb.) red snapper, cleaned, head and tail left on
1/4 cup cornstarch
Freshly ground pepper
Vegetable oil

Sauce:
1 (8-oz.) can pineapple chunks, juice pack
2 tablespoons low-sodium ketchup
1/3 cup packed brown sugar
2 teaspoons cornstarch
3 tablespoons vegetable oil
1 small onion, cut into wedges
2 garlic cloves, crushed
1/2 green bell pepper, cut into strips
1/2 red bell pepper, cut into strips
1 tomato, peeled, cut into wedges
1 tablespoon white-wine vinegar
1 teaspoon grated gingerroot, if desired

To garnish:
Cilantro leaves
Green-onion curls, page 31

---

1. Pat fish dry with paper towels. Coat with cornstarch. Season with pepper. Heat 1 inch oil in a large skillet over medium heat. Add coated fish. Fry, turning once, until golden brown and fish turns from opaque to transparent, about 15 minutes total cooking time. Place on a warm platter; keep warm.
2. To make sauce, drain pineapple, reserving juice. In a small bowl, combine ketchup, sugar and cornstarch; set aside.
3. Heat oil in a medium saucepan. Add onion and garlic; sauté until soft and transparent, 5 minutes. Add bell peppers, tomato and pineapple; cook until bell pepper is limp; remove with a slotted spoon. Add ketchup mixture to saucepan; stir in reserved pineapple juice and vinegar. Cook, stirring, until sauce thickens. Stir in gingerroot, if desired. Stir vegetable mixture back into sauce.
4. Pour sauce over cooked fish; garnish with cilantro leaves and green-onion curls. Makes 4 servings.

Variation
Substitute individual fish steaks for whole fish. Cook fish steaks about 5 to 10 minutes or until fish turns from transparent to opaque.

About 120 mg sodium per serving.

Fish & Spinach Pie

1 lb. cod or haddock fillets, skinned
1-1/2 cups milk
1/4 cup unsalted butter or margarine
1/4 cup all-purpose flour
Freshly ground pepper
1/2 (10-oz.) pkg. frozen chopped spinach, thawed,
    drained
1 tablespoon lemon juice
1 lb. boiling potatoes, cooked without salt, drained
Ground nutmeg
1 egg, beaten

*This unusual pie combines fish and spinach in a rich
sauce.*

1. Poach fish in milk in a medium skillet until fish turns
from transparent to opaque, 5 to 8 minutes. Strain cooking
liquid; set aside.
2. Cool fish slightly. Discard any bones. Flake fish; set
aside.
3. Melt 3 tablespoons butter or margarine in a medium
saucepan. Stir in flour. Cook, stirring, 2 minutes. Slowly
stir in cooking liquid until thoroughly blended. Cook,
stirring constantly, until sauce is smooth and thickened.
Stir in pepper, spinach, lemon juice and flaked fish.
4. Lightly grease a 1-quart baking dish. Spoon filling into
greased dish.
5. Preheat oven to 400F (205C). Mash potatoes. Season
with remaining 1 tablespoon butter or margarine and
nutmeg. Beat in egg. Spoon mashed potatoes over filling.
6. Bake in preheated oven until potatoes are golden
brown and filling is bubbly, 25 to 30 minutes. Makes 4
servings.

About 155 mg sodium per serving.

Baked Trout with Rosemary

4 (6- to 8-oz.) boned trout, head and tails left on
1 tablespoon unsalted butter or margarine
4 rosemary sprigs
Freshly ground pepper

To garnish:
1 lemon, cut into wedges

1. Preheat oven to 400F (205C). Grease a 13'' x 9'' baking
pan. Pat fish dry with paper towels. Make 3 slashes on
each side with a sharp knife; place fish in greased pan.
2. Reserve tips from each rosemary sprig for garnish. Place
remaining sprigs inside fish. Season with pepper.
3. Bake in preheated oven until fish turns from transparent to opaque, 20 minutes.
4. Place fish on a platter; remove rosemary sprigs from
inside fish. Garnish with rosemary tips and lemon
wedges. Makes 4 servings.

About 110 mg sodium per serving.

Left to right: South African Pickled Fish, Sweet & Sour Fish

Chicken & Poultry

Gingered Chicken

1-1/2 lbs. boneless chicken breasts, skinned, cut into
  1/2-inch wide strips
1 teaspoon sugar
1/4 cup sesame oil
1 (3-inch) piece gingerroot, cut into slivers
1/2 cup water
1/4 lb. mushrooms
2 tablespoons brandy
1 teaspoon low-sodium soy sauce
2 teaspoons cornstarch blended with 3 tablespoons
  water
Freshly ground pepper

To garnish:
Cilantro leaves

Despite the unusual amount of ginger, the flavor goes beautifully with the chicken and mushrooms and does not predominate.

1. In a medium bowl, combine chicken and sugar. Let stand 20 to 30 minutes. Drain chicken; discard any liquid.
2. Heat oil in a large skillet or wok over medium-high heat. Add gingerroot; stir-fry until slivers start to brown. Add chicken in batches; stir-fry about 3 minutes. Stir in water and mushrooms. Reduce heat. Cover and simmer until chicken is tender, about 5 minutes.
3. Add brandy and soy sauce to cornstarch mixture; stir. Add brandy mixture to chicken mixture. Bring to a boil. Stir constantly until sauce thickens. Season with pepper.
4. Spoon into a serving dish; garnish with cilantro. Makes 6 servings.

Variation
Substitute 1 pound scallops for chicken. Stir-fry until scallops turn from transparent to opaque, 3 to 4 minutes.

About 140 mg sodium per serving.

Chicken with Chilies

1-1/2 lbs. boneless chicken breasts, skinned
1 teaspoon sugar
3 fresh red chilies, seeded
4 almonds, unsalted
1 lemongrass stem, sliced
1 teaspoon ground fenugreek
1 (1-inch) piece gingerroot, coarsely chopped
6 green onions, sliced
4 garlic cloves, crushed
1/4 cup vegetable oil
1/2 cup water

To garnish:
Sliced green onions

Use red, not green, chilies for color.

1. Cut each chicken breast lengthwise into 8 pieces. In a medium bowl, combine chicken and sugar.
2. In a blender, combine chilies, almonds, lemongrass, fenugreek and 1/2 of gingerroot. Process until pureed. Spoon into a small bowl.
3. Add remaining gingerroot, green onions and garlic to blender. Process until pureed.
4. Heat oil in a deep skillet or wok. Add chili mixture; fry 1 to 2 minutes, stirring. Add onion mixture; fry 1 to 2 minutes, stirring constantly.
5. Drain chicken; discard any liquid. Add chicken pieces; turn in sauce until well coated. Add water. Reduce heat. Cover and simmer until chicken is tender, about 5 minutes.
6. Spoon into a serving dish. Garnish with green onions. Makes 6 servings.

About 102 mg sodium per serving.

Top to bottom: Chicken with Chilies, Gingered Chicken

Curried Chicken Livers

1 lb. chicken livers
2 tablespoons unsalted butter or margarine
1 small onion, finely chopped
2 teaspoons Hot Curry Powder, page 75
1 tablespoon Worcestershire sauce
2 tablespoons red-currant jelly
1/2 cup water
Freshly ground pepper
1/2 cup half and half
1 tablespoon lemon juice

To garnish:
Chopped parsley

---

1. Rinse livers; pat dry with paper towels.
2. Melt butter or margarine in a large skillet. Add livers; sauté until browned, about 5 minutes. Remove livers; set aside.
3. Add onion to juices remaining in skillet. Stir in curry powder, Worcestershire sauce and jelly; cook 1 to 2 minutes, stirring. Add water and pepper; simmer 5 minutes.
4. Remove sauce from heat. Add 3 tablespoons sauce to half and half. Pour mixture back into skillet. Return to heat.
5. Add browned livers to sauce; heat through. Do not boil. Add lemon juice.
6. Spoon into a serving dish. Sprinkle with parsley. Makes 4 servings.

About 158 mg sodium per serving.

Sesame Chicken

1 (3-lb.) chicken, quartered
1/2 cup sesame seeds, toasted
1/4 cup vegetable oil
1 medium onion, finely chopped
1 garlic clove, crushed
1 (1-inch) piece gingerroot, grated
1/2 teaspoon chili powder or red (cayenne) pepper
1/2 cup fresh low-sodium-bread crumbs

Serve chicken with a bowl of plain yogurt and a tomato-and-cucumber salad.

1. Preheat oven to 375F (190C). Lightly grease a 13" x 9" baking pan. Place chicken quarters skin-side down in greased baking pan.
2. In a small bowl, combine 1/4 cup sesame seeds, oil, onion, garlic, gingerroot and chili powder or cayenne. Spoon mixture evenly over chicken pieces.
3. Cook in preheated oven 30 minutes; turn chicken pieces over. Baste with pan juices.
4. In a small bowl, combine remaining 1/4 cup sesame seeds and bread crumbs. Sprinkle over chicken. Bake until juices run clear when chicken is pierced, 30 minutes. Makes 6 servings.

About 130 mg sodium per serving.

Chicken Rendang

1 (3-lb.) chicken, cut into 8 pieces
1 teaspoon sugar
1 cup shredded coconut
1 medium onion
2 garlic cloves, crushed
1 (1-inch) piece gingerroot
1 to 2 lemongrass stems or a few lemon-peel strips
5 tablespoons vegetable oil
2 to 4 teaspoons chili powder
1 cup Coconut Milk, page 76

---

1. Preheat oven to 375F (190C). Sprinkle chicken pieces with sugar; set aside.
2. Heat coconut in a heavy skillet until dry, golden and crisp, turning constantly to prevent burning. This will take several minutes. In a blender or food processor fitted with the steel blade; process hot coconut to an oily paste. Scrape into a small bowl; set aside.
3. In a blender or food processor fitted with the steel blade, process onion, garlic, gingerroot and lower 2 inches of lemongrass stems or lemon peel to a paste.
4. Heat oil in a large saucepan or wok over medium heat. Add onion mixture; cook 2 to 3 minutes, stirring. Reduce heat. Stir in chili powder to taste; cook 2 to 3 minutes, stirring constantly.
5. Spoon coconut cream from coconut milk; add to pan. Heat until hot. Add chicken; turn to coat with spice mixture.
6. Pour in remaining coconut milk, stirring constantly to prevent curdling. Add top part of lemongrass stems. Cover and simmer until chicken is almost tender, 35 to 40 minutes.
7. Before serving, stir in coconut paste to thicken sauce. Cook 15 minutes, stirring occasionally. Remove lemongrass. Makes 6 servings.

About 130 mg sodium per serving.

Chicken Saté

1-1/2 lbs. boneless chicken breasts, skinned, cut into
   1-inch cubes
1 teaspoon brown sugar
Cucumber chunks
Onion chunks

Marinade:
1/2 teaspoon cumin seeds
1/2 teaspoon fennel seeds
1/2 teaspoon coriander seeds
1 medium onion, sliced
1 garlic clove, crushed
1 lemongrass stem, trimmed, lower 2 inches sliced
3 cashews or almonds
1/2 teaspoon ground turmeric

Peanut Sauce:
2/3 cup unsalted roasted peanuts
1 medium onion, sliced
2 garlic cloves, crushed
6 cashews or almonds, unsalted
2 lemongrass stems, lower 2 inches sliced
3 tablespoons peanut oil
2 to 3 teaspoons chili powder
1 cup Coconut Milk, page 76
4 to 5 tablespoons lemon juice
1 tablespoon brown sugar

1. Soak 18 to 20 bamboo skewers in water at least 2 hours. Sprinkle chicken with brown sugar; set aside.
2. To make marinade, heat cumin seeds, fennel seeds and coriander seeds in a heavy skillet over medium heat. Grind or pound to a powder.
3. In a blender or food processor fitted with the steel blade, process onion, garlic, unsliced lemongrass and nuts to a paste. In a medium bowl, combine onion mixture, ground spices and turmeric. Add chicken; stir until coated with mixture. Cover and refrigerate at least 4 hours. Thread marinated chicken on skewers. Discard excess marinade.
4. To make sauce, grind peanuts until coarse and still gritty. Set aside. In a blender or food processor fitted with the steel blade, process onion, garlic, nuts and lower lemongrass sliced stems. Process to a puree.
5. Heat oil in a medium saucepan over medium heat. Add onion mixture; sauté 2 to 3 minutes, stirring. Add chili powder; cook 2 minutes, stirring.
6. Stir in coconut milk; bring to a boil. Reduce heat. Add lemon juice, sugar and ground peanuts; cook until sauce thickens, stirring. Keep warm.
7. To cook saté, place oven rack 4 to 6 inches below heat source. Grease a broiler-pan rack. Place skewers of chicken on broiler-pan rack. Broil under preheated broiler until golden brown and chicken is cooked through.
8. Serve on a large platter with cucumber and onion. Serve sauce separately. Makes 6 servings.

About 112 mg sodium per serving.

Top to bottom: Chicken Saté, Chicken Rendang

Home-Style Tandoori Chicken

1 (3-lb.) chicken
Juice of 1/2 lemon
8 cardamom pods
2 teaspoons cumin seeds
1 teaspoon fennel seeds
2 teaspoons grated gingerroot or 1 teaspoon ground
    ginger
2 or 3 garlic cloves, crushed
1 teaspoon chili powder
1/2 cup plain yogurt
2 tablespoons unsalted butter or margarine

To garnish:
Cilantro leaves

To serve:
Warm pita bread

The chicken may look overcooked because of the high cooking temperature but it will be juicy and delicious.

1. Wipe chicken with paper towels. Remove wing tips; cut chicken in half lengthwise through backbone and breast. Place skin-side up in a large baking pan.
2. Using a small sharp knife, make several cuts in chicken; rub in lemon juice.
3. Split open cardamom pods; remove seeds. Place cardamom seeds, cumin seeds and fennel seeds in a heavy skillet. Cook over a medium heat 1 to 2 minutes to bring out flavor of spices. Blend or grind to a powder; set aside.
4. In a small bowl, combine gingerroot or ginger and garlic. Stir in ground spices and chili powder.
5. Stir in yogurt. Spread chicken halves with yogurt mixture. Cover and refrigerate 5 to 6 hours.
6. Preheat oven to 425F (220C). Dot chicken with butter or margarine. Bake, uncovered, in preheated oven, basting twice in first 30 minutes. Cook until chicken is tender and juices run clear when chicken is pierced, about 1 hour total cooking time.
7. Cut chicken halves in pieces. Garnish with cilantro leaves. Serve with pita bread. Makes 6 servings.

About 140 mg sodium per serving without bread.
About 220 mg sodium per serving with 1 pita-bread round.

Clockwise from top right: Mild Curried Seafood, page 18; Home-Style Tandoori Chicken; Lamb Korma, page 48

Chicken-Stuffed Tomatoes

2 cups small shell or elbow macaroni, cooked without salt, drained
2 cups cubed cooked chicken
1/2 cup diced celery
1/2 cup minced green bell pepper
3 tablespoons finely chopped onion
1/2 cup Mayonnaise, page 77
1/2 cup plain yogurt
White pepper
Lemon juice, if desired
Lettuce leaves
4 large tomatoes

To garnish:
Parsley sprigs

1. In a medium bowl, combine cooked macaroni, chicken, celery, bell pepper and onion; set aside.
2. In a small bowl, combine mayonnaise, yogurt and white pepper. Stir mayonnaise mixture into macaroni mixture; toss to coat all ingredients. Cover and refrigerate until chilled.
3. Arrange lettuce leaves on 4 individual plates. Place a tomato, stem-end down, on each lettuce-lined plate. Cut tomato into 6 wedges, cutting almost through. Spread wedges apart. Divide chilled salad among tomatoes. Garnish with parsley sprigs. Makes 4 servings.

About 102 mg sodium per serving.

Green-Onion Curls

Trim both ends of green onion so that stem measures about 3 inches long. Use a sharp knife to shred green tops to within 1 inch of white stem. Put onions into a mixture of cold water and ice cubes 1 hour. Drain; pat dry with paper towels before using. Onions can remain in water several hours.

Turkey & Bean Bake

2 tablespoons unsalted butter or margarine
1 tablespoon vegetable oil
1 lb. turkey-breast fillets, diced
1 cup dried red kidney beans, cooked without salt
1 cup dried lima beans, cooked without salt
1 large onion, sliced
1 garlic clove, crushed
1 red bell pepper, chopped
1 tablespoon all-purpose flour
1/2 cup white wine
4 medium tomatoes, chopped
1/2 cup water
1/2 teaspoon low-sodium chicken-bouillon granules
1 teaspoon ground ginger
1 teaspoon low-sodium soy sauce
Freshly ground black pepper

1. Preheat oven to 350F (175C). Grease a 3-quart casserole dish.
2. Heat butter or margarine and oil in a large skillet over medium heat. Add turkey; sauté until lightly browned. With a slotted spoon, transfer turkey to greased casserole dish.
3. Add beans to turkey; set aside.
4. Add onion and garlic to fat remaining in skillet; sauté until onion is soft. Add bell pepper; cook 2 minutes.
5. Stir in flour; cook, stirring, 2 minutes. Stir in wine, tomatoes, water and bouillon granules; bring to a boil. Stir in ginger and soy sauce.
6. Add boiling tomato mixture to turkey and beans. Season with black pepper. Cover casserole. Bake in preheated oven until hot and bubbly, 1 hour. Makes 6 servings.

About 105 mg sodium per serving.

Roast Chicken with Tarragon

1 (3-lb.) chicken
1/4 cup Tarragon Butter, page 77, room temperature
Freshly ground pepper
1 lemon, halved

To garnish:
Tarragon sprigs

1. Preheat oven to 375F (190C). Pat chicken dry with paper towels. Place your hand under skin at neck end to ease skin away from breast and thigh meat.
2. Spread 1/2 of butter under skin and remaining 1/2 in body cavity. Replace neck flap; secure with small skewers. Sprinkle chicken with pepper.
3. Roast in preheated oven until chicken is golden brown, about 1-1/2 hours, basting once or twice with pan juices during cooking.
4. Squeeze juice from 1 lemon half over chicken breast; roast 10 minutes or until juices run clear when chicken is pierced.
5. Cut remaining lemon half in wedges. Place chicken on a platter. Garnish with lemon wedges and tarragon. Makes 6 servings.

About 125 mg sodium per serving.

Baked Turkey Cutlets with Orange Sauce

1 cup orange juice
1 tablespoon dry vermouth
1 garlic clove, crushed
Freshly ground pepper
6 turkey-breast cutlets (about 1-1/4 lbs. total)
1/2 cup orange marmalade

To garnish:
1 (11-oz.) can mandarin-orange sections, drained

1. To make marinade, in a small bowl, combine orange juice, vermouth, garlic and pepper. Place turkey in a single layer in a glass 13" x 9" baking dish; pour marinade over turkey. Cover and refrigerate several hours or overnight.
2. Preheat oven to 350F (175C). Remove cover from dish; spoon some marmalade on top of each turkey cutlet.
3. Bake, uncovered, 30 minutes or until turkey is tender, basting occasionally with marinade.
4. Place turkey on a serving platter. Strain juices into small pitcher or gravyboat; serve separately. Garnish turkey with orange sections. Makes 6 servings.

About 80 mg sodium per serving.

Crab-Stuffed Chicken Rolls with Wild Rice

8 boneless chicken-breast halves, skinned (about 1-1/4 lbs. total)
Freshly ground black pepper
1/4 lb. crabmeat
1/2 cup reduced-sodium-bread crumbs
1 teaspoon dried leaf tarragon
1 green onion, finely chopped
1/4 cup finely chopped green or red bell pepper
3 tablespoons unsalted butter or margarine
1/4 lb. mushrooms, sliced
1 green onion, sliced
1/4 cup brandy
1-1/4 cups Unsalted Chicken Stock, page 79, or 1-1/4 cups water and 1-1/4 teaspoons low-sodium chicken-bouillon granules
2 cups hot cooked wild rice
1/2 cup shredded reduced-sodium Swiss cheese (2 oz.)
3/4 teaspoon cornstarch
2 tablespoons water

The amount of crab is enough to add flavor but not a lot of additional sodium.

1. Place chicken between sheets of plastic wrap. Pound to 1/4 inch thick. Season with black pepper. Set aside.
2. In a medium bowl, combine crabmeat, bread crumbs, tarragon, finely chopped green onion and bell pepper. Divide mixture among pounded chicken breasts. Roll up to enclose stuffing. Secure with kitchen string or wooden picks.
3. Melt butter or margarine in a large skillet over medium heat. Add chicken rolls; sauté until browned. Remove chicken rolls; keep warm. Add mushrooms and sliced onion to skillet; sauté 2 minutes.
4. Return rolls to skillet. Add brandy and stock. Bring to a boil; reduce heat. Cover; simmer 20 minutes or until chicken is tender and juices run clear when pierced with a fork.
5. Spoon hot rice into a serving dish. Arrange chicken rolls over rice, reserving cooking liquid in skillet. Sprinkle chicken rolls with cheese. Cover and keep warm.
6. In a small bowl, combine cornstarch and water. Stir cornstarch mixture into cooking liquid. Cook, stirring constantly, until slightly thickened. Spoon some sauce over chicken rolls. Serve remaining sauce separately. Makes 8 servings.

About 150 mg sodium per serving.

Crab-Stuffed Chicken Rolls with Wild Rice

Fried Chicken with Herbs

1. Pat chicken dry with paper towels. Spread skin with a mixture of Tarragon and Maitre d'Hotel Butters. Refrigerate until butter is firm, about 1 hour.
2. Place flour in a plastic bag; gently toss each chilled chicken piece until coated with flour. Melt butter or margarine in a large skillet. Add floured chicken; sauté until brown on both sides.
3. Reduce heat. Stir in half and half and pepper. Simmer, covered, until chicken is tender and juices run clear when chicken is pierced, about 30 minutes.
4. Garnish with parsley and tarragon. Makes 6 servings.

About 140 mg sodium per serving.

Marinated Chicken

3 lbs. chicken pieces
1 to 2 teaspoons sugar
1 recipe Master Marinade for Chicken, page 79
1/4 cup unsalted butter or margarine

Serve with a variety of salads.

1. Using a sharp knife, cut shallow slashes in chicken skin. Place in a 13" x 9" baking dish; sprinkle chicken with sugar.
2. Pour marinade over chicken. Cover and refrigerate 4 to 6 hours, basting occasionally.
3. Preheat oven to 400F (205C). Grease a 13" x 9" baking pan. Place chicken into greased pan; dot with butter or margarine. Reserve marinade.
4. Roast in preheated oven until juices run clear when chicken is pierced, 40 minutes, basting with marinade 2 or 3 times. Makes 6 servings.

Variation
Barbecue or broil marinated chicken 20 to 25 minutes, turning often.

About 125 mg sodium per serving.

Fried Chicken with Herbs

1 (3-lb.) chicken, cut up
2 tablespoons Tarragon Butter, page 77, room
   temperature
2 tablespoons Maitre d'Hotel Butter, page 77, room
   temperature
1 cup all-purpose flour
1/4 cup unsalted butter or margarine
1/2 cup half and half
Freshly ground pepper

To garnish:
Chopped parsley
Chopped tarragon

Try spreading herb butters on fish and meats before grilling.

Chicken Curry

3 lbs. chicken pieces, skinned
1 (1-inch) piece gingerroot, chopped
2 or 3 garlic cloves, crushed
2 or 3 fresh green chilies
About 6 cilantro leaves
6 tablespoons vegetable oil
Seeds from 3 cardamom pods
1 (2-inch) cinnamon stick
2 to 3 whole cloves
12 peppercorns
2 medium onions, finely chopped
1-1/2 cups Unsalted Chicken Stock, page 79, or 1-1/2
    cups water and 1-1/2 teaspoons low-sodium
    chicken-bouillon granules

Sauce:
1 cup milk
2 tablespoons shredded coconut
1 tablespoon ground almonds
2 tablespoons cornstarch
2 tablespoons water

To garnish:
2 hard-cooked eggs, sliced
Cilantro leaves

---

*Serve with cooked rice and a selection of side dishes,
such as mango chutney, sliced bananas and green-
pepper rings.*

1. Pat chicken dry with paper towels; set aside.
2. Pound or blend gingerroot, garlic, chilies and cilantro
until reduced to a paste.
3. Heat oil in a large deep skillet. Add cardamom seeds,
cinnamon stick, cloves and peppercorns. Cook 1 minute,
stirring constantly.
4. Add onions; sauté until golden. Using a slotted spoon,
lift out onions and spices; set aside.
5. Add chicken pieces to skillet; sauté until browned on
all sides.
6. Stir gingerroot mixture into browned chicken; cook 5
minutes. Add stock and reserved onion mixture. Reduce
heat. Cover and simmer until chicken is tender, about 40
minutes.
7. To prepare sauce, place milk, coconut and almonds in a
medium saucepan. Bring to a boil. In a small bowl, combine cornstarch and water. Stir cornstarch mixture into
milk mixture; bring back to a boil, stirring constantly.
8. Stir sauce into chicken curry; cook 3 to 4 minutes to
blend flavors. Spoon into a serving dish.
9. Garnish with hard-cooked eggs and cilantro leaves.
Makes 6 servings.

About 170 mg sodium per serving.

Javanese Picnic Chicken

3 lbs. chicken pieces
2 teaspoons sugar
2 teaspoons coriander seeds
1 teaspoon chili powder
1 teaspoon ground turmeric
1-1/2 cups Coconut Milk, page 76
1/4 cup vegetable oil
1 medium onion, finely chopped
1 garlic clove, finely chopped
1 (1-inch) piece gingerroot, finely chopped
1 lemongrass stem, trimmed, bruised
3 tablespoons all-purpose flour
Vegetable oil

To serve:
Lemon wedges
Cucumber chunks

---

*Cook chicken a day ahead in spicy sauce. Drain well,
then deep fry.*

1. Pat chicken dry with paper towels. Sprinkle with sugar;
set aside.
2. Pound or grind coriander seeds. In a small bowl, combine ground coriander seeds, chili powder, turmeric and
enough coconut milk to make a paste.
3. Heat 1/4 cup oil in a deep skillet or wok. Add onion,
garlic and gingerroot; stir-fry 1 to 2 minutes.
4. Stir in spice paste and remaining coconut milk. Bring to
a boil; add chicken and lemongrass. Reduce heat. Cover
and simmer until chicken is tender, 35 to 45 minutes.
5. Spoon into a storage container; cool slightly. Cover and
refrigerate overnight.
6. Lift chicken pieces from sauce; discard sauce. Pat
chicken dry with paper towels. Dust dried chicken lightly
with flour. Heat 3 inches oil in a deep pan to 360F (180C)
or until a 1-inch bread cube turns golden brown in 60
seconds. Add floured chicken; fry until crisp and golden
brown, 6 to 8 minutes.
7. Serve with lemon wedges and cucumber chunks.
Makes 6 servings.

About 130 mg sodium per serving.

Left to right: Cold Curried Chicken, Middle Eastern Picnic Chicken

Middle Eastern Picnic Chicken

1 (3-lb.) chicken
2 tablespoons vegetable oil
1 tablespoon lemon juice
1/2 teaspoon ground turmeric
Freshly ground pepper
1 cup water
1/2 lb. chicken livers
1/4 cup unsalted butter or margarine
1 teaspoon tomato paste
2 tablespoons brandy
2 tablespoons half and half
2 to 3 tablespoons chopped mixed fresh herbs, such as mint, parsley and tarragon
Grated peel and juice of 1/2 lemon
1/2 cup chopped unsalted pistachios
Sesame Loaf, page 70, or other reduced-sodium 9-inch round loaf

1. Pat chicken dry with paper towels. Heat oil in a Dutch oven or large saucepan. Add chicken; sauté until chicken is browned on all sides, turning frequently. Add 1 tablespoon lemon juice, turmeric and pepper.
2. Reduce heat. Cover and cook 30 minutes, turning chicken several times. Add water; cook until tender, 45 to 60 minutes.
3. Cool chicken in pan until cool enough to handle. Skim off fat; reserve cooking liquid.
4. Remove meat from bones; discard bones and skin. Cut meat into bite-size pieces. Place chicken pieces into a medium bowl; set aside.
5. Rinse chicken livers; dry on paper towels. Melt butter or margarine in a medium skillet over medium heat. Add chicken livers; sauté until they change color. Reduce heat. Add tomato paste; cover and simmer until livers are no longer pink in centers, 6 to 8 minutes. Cool slightly; add brandy, half and half and pepper. In a blender or food processor, process liver mixture until pureed.
6. Stir herbs, lemon peel, lemon juice, nuts and reserved cooking liquid into chicken pieces.
7. Cut a slice from top of loaf; remove soft bread from inside bottom and lid, leaving a 1-inch shell as shown

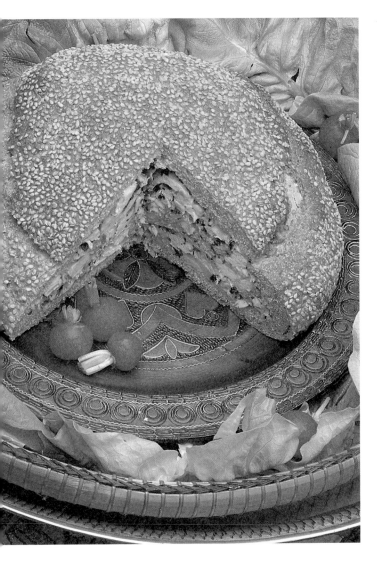

Sauce:
2 tablespoons vegetable oil
2 medium onions, finely chopped
2 tablespoons Hot or Mild Curry Powder, page 75
1 cup white wine
1 (1-lb.) can apricot halves, drained
1-1/2 cups Mayonnaise, page 77
Juice of 1 large lemon
1/2 cup whipping cream

To garnish:
1 cup sliced almonds, toasted
Cilantro or parsley sprigs

---

1. Place chicken, giblets, pepper, carrot, celery, bouquet garni and enough water barely to cover in a Dutch oven. Bring to a boil. Reduce heat. Cover and simmer until chicken is tender, 1 to 1-1/2 hours.
2. Cool in liquid 30 minutes. Remove chicken. Remove meat from bones; discard skin and bones. Cut chicken meat into bite-size pieces.
3. Strain stock; skim off fat. Set aside 1/2 cup stock for sauce. Place 4 cups of remaining stock in a saucepan; bring to a boil. Add rice. Reduce heat. Cover and cook until tender and liquid is absorbed. Cool rice to room temperature.
4. To make sauce, heat oil in a medium saucepan. Add onions; sauté until softened. Add curry powder; cook 2 minutes, stirring constantly.
5. Add wine, reserved 1/2 cup stock and pepper to taste. Cook, uncovered, stirring occasionally, 10 minutes. In a blender or food processor fitted with the steel blade, process onion mixture until smooth. Add 8 apricot halves; process until pureed. Cool slightly.
6. Drain remaining apricots on paper towels; reserve for garnish. In a medium bowl, combine mayonnaise and apricot mixture. Stir in lemon juice.
7. Whip cream. Fold into mayonnaise mixture. Fold in chicken. Place rice on a large serving plate; spoon chicken mixture into center of rice. Garnish with reserved apricot halves, almonds and cilantro or parsley. Makes 10 to 12 servings.

About 160 mg sodium per serving.

1/Scoop the soft bread from bread bottom and lid.

2/Layer chicken mixture and liver mixture inside hollowed-out loaf.

opposite. Reserve soft bread for bread crumbs for another use.
8. Spoon 1/2 of chicken mixture into bottom of loaf; cover with pureed liver mixture. Add remaining chicken mixture. Top with lid; press down gently.
9. Cover closely with plastic wrap; refrigerate several hours or overnight before serving.
10. To serve, place on a wooden board; cut into 8 wedges. Makes 8 servings.

About 185 mg sodium per serving.

Cold Curried Chicken

2 (3-lb.) chickens with giblets
Freshly ground pepper
1 carrot, quartered
1 celery stalk, roughly chopped
Bouquet Garni, page 9
2 cups long-grain rice

Roast Turkey

1 (8- to 10-lb.) turkey
Stuffing:
1/4 cup unsalted butter or margarine
1 medium onion, finely chopped
2 celery stalks, finely chopped
1 garlic clove, if desired, crushed
6 cups fresh reduced-sodium-bread crumbs
1 teaspoon rubbed sage
1 teaspoon dried leaf thyme
1 teaspoon dried leaf oregano
1 teaspoon dried rosemary
Freshly ground pepper
1 egg, beaten
About 1 cup Unsalted Chicken Stock, page 79, or 1
    cup water and 1 teaspoon reduced-sodium
    chicken-bouillon granules

1. Preheat oven to 325F (165C). Remove giblets from turkey; reserve for another use.
2. To make stuffing, in a large bowl, melt butter or margarine in a medium skillet. Add onion, celery and garlic, if desired; sauté until softened, about 5 minutes.
3. In a medium bowl, combine bread crumbs, sage, thyme, oregano, rosemary, pepper and sautéed vegetables. Stir in egg. Stir in enough stock to make a moist dressing. Loosely spoon stuffing into neck and body cavity of turkey. Place turkey, breast-side up, on a rack in a roasting pan. Truss turkey as for goose opposite.
4. Roast in preheated oven until a thermometer inserted in inner thigh reaches 180F (85C) or until juices run clear when a knife is inserted between thigh and breast, about 4 hours. Cover loosely with foil if browning too rapidly.
5. Place turkey on a platter; let stand 10 to 15 minutes before carving. Makes 8 servings.

Variation
Melt one of the herbed butters, page 77. Use as a basting sauce for turkey during last 30 minutes of roasting. Make gravy from pan juices if desired.

About 170 mg sodium per serving.

Greek Chicken with Lemon Sauce

1 (3-lb.) chicken
1 carrot, sliced
1 large onion, sliced
4 thyme sprigs
1/2 teaspoon peppercorns
1/4 cup lemon juice
1-1/2 cups long-grain rice
1/2 pint whipping cream (1 cup)
2 egg yolks
Freshly ground white or black pepper

To garnish:
1/2 cup chopped walnuts
Thyme sprigs

1. Place chicken, carrot, onion, thyme, peppercorns and enough water barely to cover in a Dutch oven. Bring to a boil. Reduce heat. Cover and simmer until chicken is tender, 1 to 1-1/2 hours.
2. Cool in liquid 30 minutes. Remove chicken. Remove meat from bones; discard skin and bones. Cut chicken meat into bite-size pieces.
3. Strain stock; place 2 cups in a medium saucepan. Reserve remaining stock for cooking rice. Bring the 2 cups stock to a boil; boil until reduced by half. Cool slightly; add lemon juice.
4. Meanwhile, bring 3 cups remaining stock to a boil in a medium saucepan; add rice. Reduce heat. Cook until tender and liquid is absorbed. Cool rice.
5. In a medium bowl, beat cream and egg yolks; stir in 1/4 cup warm stock. In a medium saucepan over medium-low heat, cook cream mixture until sauce thickens, stirring. Do not boil or sauce will curdle.
6. Stir chicken pieces into sauce. Refrigerate until sauce coats chicken, about 30 minutes.
7. Spoon rice on a platter. Arrange chicken and sauce in center of rice. Cover and refrigerate until chilled.
8. Just before serving, garnish with walnuts and thyme. Makes 6 servings.

About 150 mg sodium per serving.

Roast Goose with Sage, Onion & Apple Stuffing

1 (8- to 10-lb.) goose

Stuffing:
1-1/2 lbs. Golden Delicious apples, coarsely chopped
1 onion, finely chopped
2 cups fresh reduced-sodium-bread crumbs
1 tablespoon rubbed sage
Freshly ground pepper

To garnish:
Sage sprigs

The goose is regaining popularity, but it is still advisable to order ahead. Serve with red cabbage.

1. Preheat oven to 350F (175C). Remove excess fat from inside goose. Prick skin liberally; set goose aside.

2. To make stuffing, in a medium bowl, combine apples, onion, bread crumbs, rubbed sage and pepper. Loosely fill neck and body cavities with stuffing.

3. Fasten neck skin to back of goose using skewers. Fasten body cavity with skewers; lace with string. Bring tail up between drumsticks. Tie ends of drumsticks and tail together with string. Place stuffed goose on a rack in a roasting pan.

4. Roast, uncovered, in preheated oven until skin is golden brown, 1 hour. Pour fat from bottom of roasting pan. Cover loosely with foil. Roast goose until a thermometer inserted in inner thigh reaches 180F (80C) or until juices run clear when a knife is inserted between thigh and breast, 1-3/4 to 2 hours. Pour off fat as needed during roasting.

5. Place roasted goose on a platter. Let stand 10 to 15 minutes. Remove skewers and strings. Garnish with sage sprigs. Makes 8 to 10 servings.

About 185 mg sodium per serving.

Roast Goose with Sage, Onion & Apple Stuffing

Chicken Cardamom

1 (3-lb.) chicken, cut up
Seeds from 8 cardamom pods
1/2 teaspoon fennel seeds
1/4 to 1/2 teaspoon chili powder or red (cayenne)
   pepper
1 (1-inch) piece gingerroot, grated
2 garlic cloves, minced
1/2 cup plain yogurt
2 to 3 tablespoons unsalted butter or margarine
1 tablespoon vegetable oil
1 (2-inch) cinnamon stick
4 whole cloves
1 medium onion, finely chopped
Few strands saffron soaked in 1/4 cup hot water

To garnish:
Cilantro leaves

The cardamom gives a delicious flavor to this chicken recipe. It is a winner for a busy hostess, because it requires very little last-minute attention. Serve with hot cooked rice.

1. Place chicken in a 13" x 9" baking dish; set aside.
2. In a small heavy skillet over medium heat, heat cardamom and fennel seeds until spices give off an aroma, about 2 minutes. Pound or grind to a fine powder. Add chili powder or cayenne. In a small bowl, combine spice mixture, gingerroot, garlic and yogurt.
3. Coat chicken with yogurt mixture. Cover and refrigerate about 3 hours, basting 2 or 3 times with mixture.
4. Heat butter or margarine and oil in a Dutch oven. Add cinnamon and cloves; sauté a few seconds. Add onion; sauté until soft. Add chicken, yogurt marinade and saffron with soaking water.
5. Reduce heat. Cover and simmer until chicken is tender, about 45 minutes.
6. Remove from heat; let chicken stand 10 minutes in sauce before serving. Discard cinnamon and cloves.
7. Arrange on a platter; garnish with cilantro leaves. Makes 6 servings.

About 138 mg sodium per serving.

Top to bottom: Chicken Cardamom; Barbecued Spareribs, page 57; Fish Kabobs with Coconut Marinade, page 16

Chicken Breasts with Herb & Garlic Cheese

8 (4- to 5-oz.) boneless chicken breasts, skinned
5 oz. reduced-sodium soft herb-and-garlic cheese
6 tablespoons all-purpose flour
2 eggs, beaten
3 cups fresh reduced-sodium-bread crumbs
3 tablespoons unsalted butter or margarine

To serve:
1/2 lb. green beans or 1 (10-oz.) pkg. frozen green
   beans, cooked without salt until crisp-tender
4 cups hot cooked rice, cooked without salt

Take these on a picnic or serve them as part of a buffet. Delicious served either hot or cold.

1. Preheat oven to 375F (190C). Cut each breast in half to make 2 equal fillets. Place chicken-breast halves between sheets of plastic wrap. Pound until 1/4-inch thick.
2. Divide cheese equally among pounded breast halves. Fold sides over cheese. Starting at 1 end roll up tightly. Secure with wooden pick, if necessary. Coat chicken rolls in flour. Dip floured rolls into eggs; coat in bread crumbs.
3. Melt butter or margarine in a large baking pan. Place coated rolls in melted butter or margarine. Spoon some butter or margarine over each roll. Bake, uncovered, in preheated oven until golden brown and cooked through, 35 to 40 minutes. Baste once or twice during cooking.
4. To serve, spoon rice into a large serving dish; arrange green beans around edge of rice. Arrange baked chicken rolls in center of dish. Makes 8 servings.

About 209 mg sodium per serving.

Groundnut Stew

1/4 cup vegetable oil
1 large onion, chopped
3 lbs. chicken pieces
3/4 cup unsalted peanut butter
1-1/2 cups Unsalted Chicken Stock, page 79, or 1-1/2
   cups water and 1-1/2 teaspoons low-sodium
   chicken-bouillon granules
3 large tomatoes, peeled, chopped
2 or 3 dashes hot-pepper sauce
1 to 2 teaspoons chili powder
1/2 teaspoon ground cumin

To garnish:
4 to 6 hard-cooked eggs, if desired
Paprika

A West African chicken stew, marvelous for a simple dinner party or a Sunday lunch. The sauce can also be used for leftover chicken or turkey. Serve with cooked rice, mango chutney, sliced bananas and sliced green bell peppers.

1. In a large deep skillet, heat oil. Add onion; sauté until golden brown. Remove with a slotted spoon. Add chicken; sauté until browned on all sides. Remove chicken; drain off fat.
2. Add peanut butter and stock to skillet. Return to heat; stir to make a smooth sauce.
3. Add tomatoes, hot-pepper sauce, chili powder and cumin and browned chicken. Reduce heat. Cover and simmer until chicken is tender, 1-1/4 to 1-1/2 hours.
4. Add hard-cooked eggs, if desired; cook about 5 minutes to heat through.
5. Spoon into a serving dish; dust with paprika. Makes 6 servings.

About 135 mg sodium per serving.

Chicken-Stuffed Peppers

4 large green bell peppers
1 tablespoon vegetable oil
1 large onion, chopped
1/4 lb. mushrooms, sliced
1/4 cup chopped pecans
1 cup diced, cooked chicken
1 cup cooked rice, cooked without salt
Freshly ground black pepper
Hot-pepper sauce
1 tablespoon chopped parsley
1/4 cup reduced-sodium cheese, if desired

---

1. Preheat oven to 350F (175C). Grease a baking dish large enough to hold bell peppers. Cut off stem end of each bell pepper. Remove and discard seeds and inner pith. If peppers do not stand straight, trim to level bottoms.
2. Heat oil in a large skillet over medium heat. Add onion; sauté until soft, 5 minutes.
3. Add mushrooms and pecans; cook 3 minutes. Stir in chicken and rice. Season with black pepper, hot-pepper sauce and parsley.
4. Fill bell peppers with rice mixture. Place in greased baking dish. Cover with foil. Bake in preheated oven until bell peppers are tender, about 1 hour. Remove foil and top each bell pepper with 1/4 of cheese, if desired. Cook until cheese melts. Makes 4 servings.

About 45 mg of sodium per serving.

Chicken Gumbo

3 tablespoons vegetable oil
1 (3-lb.) chicken, cut up
2 tablespoons unsalted butter or margarine
1 large onion, sliced
1 garlic clove, crushed
1 green bell pepper, sliced
1 tablespoon all-purpose flour
4 medium tomatoes, chopped
1 cup water
1 teaspoon low-sodium chicken-bouillon granules
1 (10-oz.) pkg. frozen okra, thawed, or 3/4 lb. fresh okra, trimmed
2 tablespoons tomato paste
Pinch of ground cloves
1 teaspoon chili powder
1 teaspoon dried leaf basil
Freshly ground black pepper

To serve:
3 to 4 cups hot cooked rice, cooked without salt

---

1. Preheat oven to 350F (175C). Grease a 3-quart casserole dish.
2. Heat oil in a large skillet over medium heat. Add chicken; sauté until golden brown. Transfer chicken to greased casserole dish.
3. Melt butter or margarine in a heavy, medium saucepan. Add onion, garlic and bell pepper; sauté until soft, 5 minutes.
4. Stir flour into vegetable mixture; gradually stir in tomatoes, water and bouillon granules. Bring to a boil, stirring frequently.
5. Thickly slice okra; add to pan. Add tomato paste, cloves, chili powder, basil and pepper. Bring to a boil, stirring.
6. Pour okra mixture oven chicken. Cover casserole. Bake in preheated oven until chicken is tender, about 1 hour.
7. To serve, spoon rice into individual bowls; top with gumbo. Makes 6 servings.

About 125 mg sodium per serving.

Barbecued Chicken, page 44, cooked on a charcoal grill

Barbecued Chicken

1 (3-lb.) chicken, cut up

Marinade:
1 medium onion, chopped
1 garlic clove, crushed
1/4 cup low-sodium ketchup
1 teaspoon low-sodium soy sauce
1 cup dry white wine
2 tablespoons brown sugar
Freshly ground pepper

1. Using a sharp knife, cut 2 or 3 slashes through skin in each chicken piece to let flavors permeate meat. Place in a shallow dish, skin-side up.
2. To make marinade, in a medium bowl, combine onion, garlic, ketchup, soy sauce, wine, sugar and pepper.
3. Pour marinade over chicken. Cover and refrigerate 8 to 12 hours, basting occasionally.
4. Preheat oven to 375F (190C). Grease a 13" x 9" baking pan. Add chicken and marinade to pan. Bake in preheated oven until chicken is tender, 35 to 40 minutes, basting several times.
5. For browner chicken, remove from sauce. Place under a preheated broiler until browned, about 10 minutes.
6. Serve hot. Makes 6 servings.

Variation
Drain chicken, reserving marinade. Cook chicken on pre-heated grill. Baste with reserved marinade during last 10 minutes of cooking.

About 160 mg sodium per serving.

Clockwise from left: Barbecued Chicken; Duck with Oriental Plum Sauce; Braised Beef, page 63

Duck with Oriental Plum Sauce

1 (16-oz.) can plums, pitted, liquid reserved
Juice of 1 lemon
Grated peel and juice of 1 orange
1/4 teaspoon ground allspice
1/4 teaspoon dry mustard
1 (5-lb.) duck
2 green onions, cut in 3-inch pieces
2 or 3 sprigs each oregano and thyme
1 teaspoon cornstarch mixed with 2 tablespoons water

To garnish:
Watercress

The Oriental plum sauce is made a day ahead.

1. In a blender or food processor fitted with the steel blade, combine plums with liquid, lemon juice, orange peel, orange juice, allspice and mustard. Process until pureed.
2. Pour puree into a quart jar or other container with a lid. Cover and refrigerate overnight.
3. The next day, preheat oven to 375F (190C). Prick duck all over to allow fat to escape during cooking. Place green onions and herbs in neck and body cavity. Truss duck as for chicken, opposite. Place on a rack in a roasting pan. Roast in preheated oven until juices run clear when duck is pierced between thigh and breast, about 2 hours. Drain fat from roasting pan as necessary.
4. Place duck on a platter. Remove trussing skewers and string. Pour plum sauce into a medium saucepan. Bring to a boil. Reduce heat. Simmer, uncovered, 10 minutes. Stir in cornstarch mixture. Cook, stirring, until slightly thickened.
5. Cut duck into 4 quarters. Discard onions and herbs. If duck skin is not crisp, place under preheated broiler until browned and crispy. Serve sauce separately. Garnish with watercress. Makes 4 servings.

About 140 mg sodium per serving.

Chicken Marrakesh

1 (3-lb.) chicken
5 tablespoons vegetable oil
1 garlic clove, crushed
1 (1-inch) piece gingerroot, cut into slivers
2 or 3 whole cloves
1 (3-inch) cinnamon stick
2 teaspoons ground turmeric
Freshly ground pepper
3 cups water
1/4 lb. almonds, ground

To garnish:
Lemon wedges
Cilantro leaves

This attractive party dish goes well with rice.

1. Pat chicken dry with paper towels; truss as shown below.
2. Heat 4 tablespoons oil in a Dutch oven. Add garlic, gingerroot, cloves, cinnamon, and 1/2 of turmeric; sauté 2 minutes, stirring. Add chicken; turn to coat with spice mixture. Place chicken, breast-side down.
3. Add pepper and water; bring to a boil. Reduce heat. Cover and simmer until chicken is tender, about 1-1/2 hours.
4. Place chicken on a platter; remove trussing strings. Keep warm.
5. Strain stock; skim off fat. Return 1-1/2 cups stock to pan; stir in ground almonds. Bring to a boil, stirring frequently. Cook, uncovered, until sauce thickens, 2 to 3 minutes. Pour almond sauce over chicken.
6. In a small bowl, combine remaining turmeric powder and oil. Drizzle over chicken and sauce. Garnish with lemon wedges and cilantro leaves. Makes 6 servings.

About 130 mg sodium per serving.

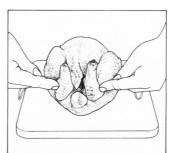

1/To truss a chicken, cut a 3- to 5-foot length of kitchen string. Place middle of string under tail. Bring string ends up, crossing over ends of drumsticks, bringing string under drumsticks.

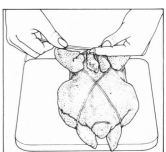

2/Bring 1 string over 1 wing and neck skin. Bring remaining end over other wing. Knot tightly.

Roast Chicken with Cherry-Orange Glaze

2 (3-lb.) chickens

Cherry-Orange Glaze:
1/2 cup cherry jam
1/2 cup orange marmalade
1/4 cup orange juice
1/2 teaspoon ground allspice

1. Preheat oven to 375F (190C). Remove giblets from chickens; reserve for another use, if desired. Rinse chickens; pat dry with paper towels. Truss chickens as directed on page 45. Place chickens on a rack in a roasting pan.
2. Roast chickens about 1-1/2 hours. Meanwhile make glaze. To make glaze, in a small bowl, combine all glaze ingredients. Brush glaze over chickens. Roast 30 minutes longer or until a thermometer inserted between thigh and breast reads 180F (80C) or until juices run clear when chicken is pierced with a fork.
3. Place chickens on a platter; let stand 10 minutes before carving. Makes 8 to 10 servings.

About 180 mg sodium per serving.

Chicken Marengo

1 (3-lb.) chicken, cut up
Freshly ground pepper
1/4 cup unsalted butter or margarine
1 large onion, sliced
2 garlic cloves, crushed
4 medium tomatoes, chopped
2 tablespoons tomato paste
1/2 cup red wine
1/4 lb. mushrooms, sliced

Serve hot over cooked pasta, if desired.

1. Preheat oven to 350 (175C). Grease a 3-quart casserole dish. Season chicken with pepper.
2. Melt butter or margarine in a large skillet over medium heat. Add chicken; sauté until golden brown. Place chicken in greased casserole dish.
3. Add onion and garlic to fat remaining in skillet; sauté until soft, 5 minutes. Stir in tomatoes, tomato paste and wine; bring to a boil.
4. Add mushrooms; cook 2 minutes. Pour tomato mixture over chicken. Cover casserole.
5. Bake in preheated oven until chicken is tender, about 1 hour. Makes 6 servings.

About 140 mg sodium per serving.

Roast Chicken with Cherry-Orange Glaze

Meat

Crown Roast of Lamb with Lemon & Mint Stuffing

1 (2-lb.) lamb crown rib roast
Freshly ground pepper

Stuffing Balls:
3 cups reduced-sodium-bread crumbs
Finely grated peel and juice of 1 lemon
2 to 3 tablespoons finely chopped mint
2 tablespoons unsalted butter or margarine, melted
2 eggs, beaten
Freshly ground pepper

To garnish:
Mint sprigs

The tips of the bones are scraped clean. During cooking, cover with a small double foil square to prevent burning.

1. Preheat oven to 350F (175C). Season roast with pepper. Place on a rack in a roasting pan. Make a firm ball of foil; press into center cavity. Cover exposed bones with foil.
2. Roast in preheated oven until lamb is to desired doneness, about 1-1/2 hours. For rare, cook to an internal temperature of 140F (60C). For medium, cook to an internal temperature of 160F (70F). For well-done, cook to an internal temperature of 170F (75C).
3. Meanwhile prepare stuffing. In a medium bowl, combine bread crumbs, lemon peel, lemon juice and mint. Add butter or margarine and enough egg to bind. Season with pepper. Roll into walnut-size balls; place around roast after first 30 minutes of roasting. Baste stuffing balls with a little pan drippings.
4. Place roast on a platter; let stand 10 minutes. Remove foil caps from bones; replace with paper frills, if desired. Remove foil ball from center; fill with baked stuffing balls. Garnish with mint sprigs. Makes 6 servings.

About 180 mg sodium per serving.

Lamb Korma

6 tablespoons unsalted butter or margarine
1 large onion, finely chopped
3 garlic cloves, crushed
1 (1-inch) piece gingerroot, cut into slivers
1 teaspoon chili powder
1 tablespoon Garam Masala, page 76
1-1/2 lbs. lamb for stew, cut into 1-inch cubes
1/2 cup plain yogurt
Few strands of saffron soaked in 1/2 cup warm water

To garnish:
Cilantro leaves

To serve:
Lemon wedges
3 cups hot cooked rice, cooked without salt

Traditionally, a korma is a dry curry, but this one is moist. Eat with chapatis (Indian bread) or rice.

1. Melt butter or margarine in a large saucepan. Add onion, garlic and gingerroot; sauté, stirring frequently, until softened.
2. Add chili powder and garam masala. Add meat in batches; cook until browned on all sides.
3. Reduce heat. Stir in yogurt. Add saffron and water; stir well.
4. Cover and simmer until meat is tender, about 1 hour. Add additional water if necessary. Or bake, covered, in a preheated 325F (165C) oven about 1-1/4 hours.
5. Garnish with cilantro. Serve with lemon wedges and rice. Makes 6 servings.

About 92 mg sodium per serving.

Top to bottom: Crown Roast of Lamb with Lemon & Mint Stuffing; Beef Rolls, page 52

Chinese-Style Pork Stew

3 fresh red chilies, seeded, or 2 to 3 teaspoons chili
   powder
3 medium onions, quartered
6 garlic cloves
6 tablespoons vegetable oil
4 lbs. fresh pork hocks, cut into 1-1/2-inch pieces
1 tablespoon lime juice
1 teaspoon low-sodium soy sauce
2 teaspoons sugar
1-1/2 cups water

To garnish:
Fresh cilantro or parsley

---

*This recipe is even better when cooked a day ahead.
Remove any fat from surface before reheating.*

1. Cut a few rings from tips of chilies; wrap and refrigerate
for garnish. Combine remaining chilies, onions and garlic
in a blender. Process until pureed. If using chili powder,
add to onion puree after processing.
2. Heat oil in a large skillet or wok. Add chili paste; cook,
stirring, 2 to 3 minutes. Do not brown. Add pork; turn to
coat with chili mixture.
3. Stir in lime juice, soy sauce, sugar and water. Reduce
heat. Cover and simmer until pork is tender, about 1 hour.
Cool quickly. Cover and refrigerate overnight.
4. Preheat oven to 325F (165C). Remove any fat from top
of stew. Pour into a casserole dish; cover. Heat in preheated oven until hot and bubbling, about 45 minutes.
5. Garnish with reserved chili rings and cilantro or parsley. Makes 6 servings.

About 140 mg sodium per serving.

Pork Chops with Sherry

4 pork chops, about 1/4 lb. each
1 cup medium dry sherry
4 bay leaves
Freshly ground pepper
2 tablespoons unsalted butter or margarine
1/4 cup red-currant jelly
2 teaspoons Dijon-style mustard

To garnish:
Parsley sprigs

---

1. Place pork chops in a shallow glass dish. Add sherry,
bay leaves and pepper.
2. Cover and marinate 1 hour. Remove pork chops, reserving marinade. Pat pork chops dry with paper towels.
3. Melt butter or margarine in a large skillet. Add pork
chops; sauté until browned on both sides, turning once.
Pour in reserved marinade. Reduce heat. Cover and simmer until pork chops are no longer pink in center and
sherry is reduced by 1/2, about 20 minutes.
4. Arrange chops in a serving dish. Whisk red-currant
jelly and mustard into remaining sherry. Stir until jelly
melts and sauce is smooth. Pour sauce over chops. Garnish with parsley sprigs. Makes 4 servings.

About 130 mg sodium per serving.

Pork Chops with Peppercorn-Cream Sauce

1/4 cup unsalted butter or margarine
2 tablespoons vegetable oil
4 pork chops, about 1/4 lb. each
1/2 cup half and half
2 teaspoons lemon juice
1-1/2 tablespoons black peppercorns, cracked
1/4 lb. mushrooms
2 tablespoons chopped parsley

---

*Peppercorns grow on a vine. Green peppercorns are pre-
served in brine and packed in small jars. They are available in delicatessens and some supermarkets. Black peppercorns are ripened in the sun. White peppercorns are
the same ripe peppercorns soaked in running water for a
week, then rubbed to remove the outer skin. White pepper
is not as pungent and aromatic as black pepper.*

1. Preheat oven to 350F (175C). Heat 2 tablespoons butter
or margarine and oil in a large skillet over medium heat.
Add pork chops; sauté 5 minutes on each side to brown.
Transfer to a large shallow casserole.
2. Skim excess fat from pan, keeping juices. Stir in cream,
then lemon juice; bring to a boil. Add peppercorns; pour
evenly over browned chops.
3. Bake, covered, in preheated oven 30 minutes. Remove
cover; bake 10 minutes or until centers of pork chops are
no longer pink in centers.
4. Meanwhile, heat remaining 2 tablespoons butter or
margarine in a medium skillet. Add mushrooms; sauté 2
to 3 minutes. Sprinkle with parsley. Serve mushrooms on
the side. Makes 4 servings.

About 110 mg sodium per serving.

Mulligatawny Soup

1 lb. beef for stew, cut into 1-inch cubes
2 lbs. beef soup bones
About 8 cups water
1 tablespoon coriander seeds
1/2 teaspoon peppercorns
1 teaspoon cumin seeds
1 teaspoon ground turmeric
6 cardamom pods, bruised lightly
2 to 3 whole cloves
4 garlic cloves, crushed
2 medium potatoes, diced
2 tablespoons unsalted butter or margarine
1 large onion, finely sliced
1 teaspoon Garam Masala, page 76, or 1 teaspoon
   Mild Curry Powder, page 75
2 cups Coconut Milk, page 76
Juice of 1 lemon

To garnish:
Cilantro leaves
Unsalted croutons sprinkled with mustard seeds or
   poppy seeds

The addition of coconut milk makes this version particularly enjoyable.

1. Place beef and bones in a large saucepan with water. Bring to a boil; skim foam from surface often.
2. Add coriander, peppercorns, cumin, turmeric, cardamom, cloves and garlic. Reduce heat. Cover and simmer until meat is tender, about 1-1/2 hours. Cool slightly.
3. Remove and discard bones. Remove meat; shred. Set aside. Strain soup; discard spices.
4. Place 6 cups stock and potatoes into pan. Bring to a boil. Reduce heat. Cover and simmer until potatoes are tender, about 10 minutes. Stir in reserved meat; set aside.
5. In a medium saucepan, melt butter or margarine. Add onion; sauté just until onion begins to color. Add garam masala or curry powder. Remove from heat; stir in coconut milk.
6. Stir onion mixture into soup. Add lemon juice; heat through. Do not boil or soup may curdle.
7. Serve in soup bowls. Top with cilantro and croutons. Makes 6 servings.

About 60 mg sodium per serving.

Top to bottom: Javanese Picnic Chicken, page 35; Fish Moolie, page 21; Mulligatawny Soup

Beef Rolls

8 thin slices of beef round steak (about 4 to 5 oz. each)
2 cups fresh reduced-sodium-bread crumbs
2 teaspoons chopped parsley
1 teaspoon chopped oregano
1 teaspoon chopped thyme
Freshly ground pepper
1 egg, beaten
5 tablespoons all-purpose flour
2 to 4 tablespoons vegetable oil
1 large onion, chopped
3 cups Unsalted Beef Stock, page 78 or 3 cups water and 1 tablespoon very low-sodium beef-bouillon granules
2 tablespoons tomato paste
3 tablespoons red wine

To garnish:
Chopped parsley

Serve with cooked carrots or broccoli and mashed potatoes.

1. Trim beef slices, if necessary; set aside. In a medium bowl, combine bread crumbs, parsley, oregano, thyme and pepper. Add enough egg to bind.
2. Spoon mixture equally over beef slices. Roll each beef slice carefully to enclose filling. Tie with kitchen string.
3. Coat rolls lightly with flour; reserve excess flour. Heat oil in a large skillet. Add floured rolls; sauté until browned on all sides. Remove from skillet with tongs.
4. Add onion to remaining oil; sauté until softened. Add remaining flour; cook 2 minutes, stirring constantly. Gradually stir in stock, tomato paste and wine. Bring to a boil, stirring constantly.
5. Return beef rolls to skillet. Reduce heat. Cover and simmer until meat is tender, 1-1/2 to 2 hours.
6. Arrange rolls on a serving plate. Sprinkle with parsley. Makes 8 servings.

About 90 mg sodium per serving.

Pork with Prunes

6 oz. pitted prunes
1-1/2 cups white wine
1 (2-inch) cinnamon stick
4 whole cloves
1 (1-lb.) pork tenderloin
5 tablespoons all-purpose flour
1/4 cup unsalted butter or margarine
1 tablespoon vegetable oil
3 tablespoons red-currant jelly
1/2 pint dairy sour cream (1 cup)
Freshly ground pepper

To garnish:
Lemon slices
Dill or fennel sprigs

Sprinkle fresh feathery dill over fish, potato or pasta salads. Fennel looks similar to dill but has a strong anise flavor.

1. In a medium saucepan, cook prunes with wine, cinnamon and cloves until tender, about 10 minutes; set aside.
2. Meanwhile, slice pork into 1/4-inch-thick slices. Coat pork slices with flour.
3. Heat butter or margarine and oil in a large skillet. Add floured pork slices; sauté until browned on both sides, turning once. Add 1/4 cup cooking liquid from prunes to skillet. Reduce heat. Cover and simmer until pork is no longer pink in center, about 10 minutes.
4. Arrange pork on a serving dish. Lift out prunes with a slotted spoon, reserving cooking liquid. Add prunes to pork; keep warm.
5. Melt red-currant jelly in a medium saucepan. Add reserved cooking liquid, discarding cinnamon and cloves. Whisk until smooth. Boil 3 to 4 minutes to reduce sauce slightly.
6. In a small bowl, combine sour cream and 2 tablespoons hot sauce. Add warmed cream mixture to remaining sauce. Reheat; do not boil. Pour sauce over pork and prunes. Garnish with lemon and dill or fennel. Makes 4 servings.

About 100 mg sodium per serving.

Roast Pork with Juniper Berries

1 (7-lb.) pork leg half
2 oranges
2 tablespoons juniper berries, crushed
2 garlic cloves, crushed
Freshly ground pepper

Serve with steamed carrots and broccoli and baked potatoes.

1. Remove skin and excess fat from pork. Score remaining fat in diamond shapes.
2. Grate peel from 1 orange. Cut oranges in half. Juice grated orange and 1/2 of remaining orange. Cut remaining half in slices for garnish; cover and refrigerate. In a small bowl, combine juniper berries, garlic, pepper and 1/2 of orange peel. Rub mixture into scored pork. Cover and refrigerate about 2 hours.
3. Preheat oven to 325F (165C). Place pork on a rack in a roasting pan. Roast in preheated oven until a thermometer inserted in thickest part reads 170F (75C) or until pork is no longer pink in center, 4 to 4-1/2 hours.
4. Place roast on a platter; cover with foil. Let stand while making sauce.
5. Skim fat from pan juices. Stir in remaining 1/2 of orange peel and orange juice. Bring to a boil, stirring.
6. Cut pork into thick slices. Garnish with orange slices. Serve sauce separately or pour around roast. Makes 10 to 12 servings.

About 115 mg sodium per serving.

Clockwise from upper left: Roast Pork with Juniper Berries; Roast Turkey, page 38; Beef Pot Roast, page 54

Beef-Tenderloin Kabobs with Béarnaise Sauce

1 lb. beef loin tenderloin, cut into 2-inch cubes
16 button mushrooms
1 green bell pepper, cut into squares
A little olive oil

Béarnaise Sauce:
2 very small onions or shallots, finely chopped
1/4 cup herb-flavored vinegar
2 tablespoons chopped fresh tarragon or 1/2 teaspoon
   dried leaf tarragon
1/2 teaspoon dry mustard
4 egg yolks
1/2 cup unsalted butter or margarine, melted
Freshly ground pepper
Lemon juice to taste
2 teaspoons chopped parsley

1. Soak 8 bamboo skewers in water at least 2 hours. Position oven rack about 6 inches from heat source. Preheat broiler.
2. Alternately thread beef, mushrooms and bell peppers on skewers. Place on a rack on a roasting pan. Brush beef and vegetables with olive oil; set aside.
3. To make sauce, combine onions or shallots, vinegar and tarragon in a small saucepan. Simmer until vinegar is reduced to 2 tablespoons. Strain into a small bowl; set aside.
4. Place bottom of a double boiler containing water over medium heat. Bring to a simmer; reduce heat to low. Place mustard and egg yolks in top of double boiler over hot water. Whisk until mixture thickens and is lemon-colored, about 5 to 6 minutes. Add butter or margarine in a slow, steady stream, whisking. Whisk in reserved vinegar mixture. Add lemon juice to taste; stir in parsley. Remove from heat; keep warm while broiling kabobs.
5. Broil kabobs under preheated broiler to desired doneness, 5 to 10 minutes. Serve at once with sauce. Makes 4 servings.

About 90 mg sodium per serving.

How to Cook Dried Beans

Sort through dried beans; discard discolored beans. Soak beans overnight in water to cover; drain. Place beans in a saucepan; cover with water. Bring to a boil. Reduce heat. Cover and simmer until tender, about 1-1/2 hours, depending on type of bean. One cup uncooked beans makes 2 cups cooked beans.

Beef Pot Roast

1 (3-1/2-lb.) beef rump roast boneless
Marinade:
1/4 cup wine vinegar
1-1/2 cups red wine
1 medium onion, sliced
1/2 teaspoon peppercorns, crushed
1 teaspoon juniper berries, crushed
6 whole cloves
Bouquet Garni, page 9
2 tablespoons vegetable oil
4 carrots, sliced
2 celery stalks, chopped
Freshly ground pepper
1/2 lb. pearl onions
1/2 cup Unsalted Beef Stock, page 78, or 1/2 cup
   water and 1/2 teaspoon very low-sodium
   beef-bouillon granules
2 tablespoons butter or margarine blended with 2
   tablespoons all-purpose flour

Serve with green vegetables and boiled potatoes.

1. Place roast in a medium stainless steel or glass bowl.
2. To make marinade, in a medium bowl, combine vinegar, wine, onion, peppercorns, juniper berries, cloves and bouquet garni. Pour over roast. Cover and refrigerate overnight, turning occasionally.
3. Lift roast from marinade, reserving marinade. Pat roast dry with paper towels. Strain marinade; set aside.
4. Heat oil in a Dutch oven. Add roast; sauté until browned on all sides, turning. Remove roast; set aside. Add carrots and celery to pan; sauté until lightly browned.
5. Return roast to pan; pour in strained marinade. Bring to a boil. Reduce heat. Cover and simmer about 1-1/2 hours.
6. Place onions into a saucepan of boiling water; boil 5 minutes. Drain; add to roast. Cook until roast and onions are tender, about 30 minutes.
7. Place roast and onions on a platter; keep warm. To make sauce, strain cooking liquid into a medium saucepan, discarding carrots and celery. Add stock.
8. Add flour-and-butter mixture to cooking liquid, a little at a time. Cook, whisking, until sauce thickens slightly. Serve sauce separately. Makes 8 servings.

About 145 mg sodium per serving.

Chili con Carne

1-1/2 lbs. lean ground beef
2 medium onions, finely chopped
2 garlic cloves, crushed
1 to 2 teaspoons chili powder
1/2 teaspoon cumin seeds
1-1/2 teaspoons chopped fresh oregano or 1/2
 teaspoon dried leaf oregano
1 tablespoon tomato paste
3 medium tomatoes, finely chopped
2 cups Unsalted Beef Stock, page 78, or 2 cups water
 and 2 teaspoons very low-sodium beef-bouillon
 granules
Freshly ground pepper
1 (15-oz.) can red-kidney beans, drained

To garnish:
Chopped chives

This Southwestern dish has many versions. Vary the herbs and spices to find your favorite.

1. Brown meat in a large saucepan or Dutch oven, stirring to break up meat.
2. Add onions and garlic to meat; cook until softened. Drain off excess fat. Add chili powder to taste, cumin and oregano. Stir in tomato paste, tomatoes, stock and pepper.
3. Bring to a boil. Reduce heat. Cover and simmer until onions are tender and mixture is slightly thickened. Stir in beans; simmer 15 minutes.
4. Ladle into individual bowls. Sprinkle with chives. Makes 6 servings.

About 95 mg sodium per serving.

Chili con Carne

Marinated Lamb Roast

1 (4-1/2 lb.) leg-of-lamb half
1 recipe Cooked Wine Marinade, page 78
3 tablespoons vegetable oil
3 carrots, sliced
4 onions, sliced
6 tablespoons all-purpose flour
1-1/2 cups Unsalted Beef Stock, page 78, or 1-1/2 cups
    water and 1-1/2 teaspoons very low-sodium
    beef-bouillon granules
1/4 cup red-currant jelly, warmed

1. Place lamb in a large stainless steel or glass bowl. Add marinade. Cover and refrigerate 3 days, turning.
2. Preheat oven to 325F (165C). Remove lamb from marinade, reserving marinade. Pat lamb dry with paper towels. Pour oil into a roasting pan; add carrots and onions. Toss to coat with oil.
3. Place marinated lamb on vegetables. Roast in preheated oven to desired doneness, 1-3/4 to 2-1/4 hours. For rare, cook to an internal temperature of 140F (60C). For medium, cook to an internal temperature of 160F (70F). For well-done, cook to an internal temperature of 170F (75C). Baste occasionally with reserved marinade.
4. Place roasted lamb on a platter. To make gravy, remove carrots and onions with a slotted spoon; place in a serving bowl. Skim fat from pan juices. Stir in flour. Cook, stirring, 3 minutes. Gradually stir in remaining marinade, stock and red-currant jelly.
5. Serve with carrots and onions from roasting pan. Makes 8 servings.

About 160 mg sodium per serving.

Left to right: Lamb Persille, Zucchini Pie, page 72

Lamb Persille

2 (2- to 3-lb.) lamb rib roasts, chined
1/4 cup Mint Butter, page 77
Freshly ground pepper

Herb Mixture:
1-1/2 cups fresh low-sodium-bread crumbs
2 teaspoons chopped parsley
2 teaspoons chopped mint
2 teaspoons chopped fresh cilantro or 1/2 teaspoon
   crushed coriander seeds
Freshly ground pepper
Grated peel of 1/2 lemon
4 to 6 tablespoons unsalted butter or margarine,
   melted

To garnish:
Watercress

1. Preheat oven to 350F (175C). Pat roasts dry with paper towels. Spread Mint Butter on fat side. Season with pepper; place, butter-side up, in a roasting pan. Roast in preheated oven about 1 hour, basting once or twice.
2. Meanwhile prepare herb mixture. Place bread crumbs, herbs, lemon peel and pepper in a bowl. Stir in melted butter or margarine.
3. Remove roasts from oven. Increase oven temperature to 400F (205C).
4. Press herb mixture on top of meat. Roast until crumbs are browned and roasts are cooked to desired doneness, 20 minutes. For rare, cook to an internal temperature of 140F (60C). For medium, cook to an internal temperature of 160F (70F). For well-done, cook to an internal temperature of 170F (75C).
5. Arrange roasts on a platter. Garnish with watercress. To serve, cut down between bones with a sharp knife so that everyone get chops with a crisp coating. Makes 6 servings.

About 155 mg sodium per serving.

Barbecued Spareribs

2 lbs. pork spareribs

Marinade:
3 to 6 garlic cloves, crushed
5 to 6 fresh red chilies or 1 to 2 teaspoons chili
   powder
1 cup pineapple juice
2 tablespoons wine vinegar
2 teaspoons cornstarch
1/4 cup packed brown sugar
2-1/2 tablespoons dry sherry
1 teaspoon low-sodium soy sauce

To garnish:
Green-onion curls, page 31

Serve finger bowls of water containing a slice of lemon or a few flower petals. Or pass small damp towels after your guests have finished eating.

1. Place spareribs in a 13" x 9" baking dish.
2. In a blender or food processor fitted with the steel blade, process garlic, chilies or chili powder, pineapple juice, vinegar, cornstarch, brown sugar, sherry and soy sauce until pureed.
3. Pour mixture over spare ribs. Cover and refrigerate overnight, basting occasionally.
4. Preheat oven to 375F (190C). Drain ribs, discarding marinade. Arrange spare ribs on racks in 2 roasting pans. Pour a little water into base of each pan to catch drips and to prevent smoking.
5. Roast ribs in preheated oven until browned and no longer pink near bones, 1 to 1-1/4 hours. Turn once or twice during cooking.
6. Serve hot. Cut ribs apart for easier eating. Garnish with green-onion curls. Makes 4 servings.

About 120 mg sodium per serving.

Chinese Fried Rice

5 tablespoons vegetable oil
1 egg, beaten
4 green onions, sliced
3 garlic cloves, crushed
1/2 lb. cold roast pork, shredded
4 Chinese dried mushrooms, soaked in water 1 hour,
   drained, sliced
3 cups cold cooked rice, cooked without salt
1 teaspoon low-sodium soy sauce
Freshly ground pepper
1 cup fresh green peas
1 red chili, chopped, if desired

To garnish:
Cilantro leaves
Shredded lettuce leaves

The Chinese mushrooms are available in Oriental markets and some supermarkets. They give an authentic flavor to this recipe.

1. Heat 1 tablespoon oil in a small skillet. Add egg; cook until set. Remove from skillet; roll up. Cut into 5 strips; set aside.
2. Heat 2 tablespoons oil in a large skillet or wok. Add green onions; stir-fry until softened. Remove with a slotted spoon; set aside.
3. Add garlic, pork and mushrooms; stir-fry 1 to 2 minutes. Remove with a slotted spoon; set aside.
4. Add 2 tablespoons oil to skillet or wok; heat until hot. Add rice; stir-fry until all grains are coated with oil and rice is hot. Add soy sauce, pepper and reserved pork mixture. Stir-fry until combined. Add peas, and chili, if desired; stir-fry until heated through.
5. Spoon into a serving dish. Garnish with cilantro and lettuce. Makes 4 servings.

About 85 mg sodium per serving.

Lamb Chops with Herb Butter

8 lamb loin chops, 1-inch thick
Freshly ground pepper
1/4 cup herbed butter of your choice, page 77
8 reduced-sodium bread slices, crusts removed,
  toasted

Vary the flavor of the broiled chops by choosing your favorite herbs for the Herb Butter.

1. Place oven rack 6 inches from heat source. Preheat broiler. Season chops with pepper; place on a rack in a broiler pan.
2. Cook under preheated broiler 4 to 5 minutes on first side. Turn chops. Broil 4 to 5 minutes on second side or to desired doneness.
3. Top each chop with 1/8 of butter; place chops on toasted bread slices. Makes 4 servings.

About 170 mg sodium per serving.

Clockwise from top left: Pita Bread, page 68; Cucumber-Yogurt Salad, page 71; Moroccan Kebabs

Moroccan Kabobs

1-3/4 lb. lean ground lamb
2 lamb kidneys

Spice Marinade:
2 tablespoons cumin seeds
1 (1-inch) piece gingerroot, sliced or 1 teaspoon
  ground ginger
1 medium onion, sliced
3 to 4 garlic cloves
2 tablespoons water
1 teaspoon chili powder
1 teaspoon ground turmeric
3 to 4 tablespoons chopped fresh parsley
Freshly ground pepper

To serve:
Hot Pita Bread, page 68

Try these kabobs for a casual lunch or barbecue party. Serve a selection of accompaniments, such as radishes, green onions and cucumbers.

1. Form meat into walnut-size meatballs. Cut kidneys in half; remove white core. Cut kidneys into 1-inch pieces. Place meatballs and kidney pieces in a medium bowl.
2. To make marinade, pound or blend cumin seeds into a powder. In a blender or food processor fitted with the steel blade, process gingerroot or ginger, onion, garlic and water until pureed. Add powdered cumin seeds, chili powder, turmeric, parsley and pepper; process until blended.
3. Add spice mixture to meatballs and kidney pieces. Stir gently to coat. Cover and refrigerate at least 2 hours, stirring occasionally. Soak 16 bamboo skewers in water while meat is marinating. Or use metal skewers.
4. Light a charcoal fire in an outdoor grill. Position rack 6 inches above heat. Thread marinated meatballs and kidneys onto skewers. When coals are evenly hot, place skewers on grill. Grill until cooked to desired doneness, turning frequently, 10 to 12 minutes.
5. Serve with pita bread and suggested accompaniments, above. Makes 8 servings.

About 175 mg sodium per serving with 1 pita round.

Turkish-Style Stuffed Lamb

1 (3-lb.) boned leg-of-lamb half
Freshly ground pepper

Stuffing:
1 tablespoon unsalted butter or margarine
1 small onion, finely chopped
1/4 cup pine nuts
1/4 cup long-grain rice
1/2 cup water
1 teaspoon coriander seeds, crushed
Freshly grated nutmeg
Grated peel and juice of 1 orange
1/4 cup raisins

To garnish:
Cilantro leaves

1. Sprinkle lamb inside and out with pepper; set aside.
2. To make stuffing, melt butter or margarine in a medium saucepan. Add onion; sauté until softened. Add pine nuts and rice. Stir well; add water. Bring to a boil. Reduce heat. Cover and simmer until rice is almost tender, about 10 minutes.
3. Preheat oven to 350F (175C). Remove rice from heat; stir in coriander, nutmeg, 1/2 of orange peel and raisins. Cool to room temperature. Use mixture to fill cavity of lamb. Reshape lamp; tie with kitchen string.
4. Roast in preheated oven until lamb is to desired doneness, 1-1/2 to 2 hours. For rare, cook to an internal temperature of 140F (60C). For medium, cook to an internal temperature of 160F (70F). For well-done, cook to an internal temperature of 170F (75C). Place roast on a platter; remove string. Keep warm.
5. Skim fat from pan juices; pour juices into a small saucepan. Add remaining orange peel and orange juice. Heat until hot. Pour sauce into a small pitcher or gravy boat.
6. Carve lamb into thick slices; garnish with lots of cilantro. Serve sauce separately. Makes 8 servings.

About 85 mg sodium per serving.

Marinated-Lamb Barbecue

12 lamb chops, about 1/4 lb. each, 1 inch thick
3/4 cup dry white wine
2 tablespoons olive oil
2 garlic cloves, crushed
2 tablespoons mango chutney
1 tablespoon Hot or Mild Curry Powder, page 75
2 tablespoons brown sugar
5 or 6 rosemary sprigs
Freshly ground pepper

To garnish:
Parsley sprigs

1. Place lamb in a shallow dish. In a small bowl, combine wine, olive oil and garlic. Stir in mango chutney, curry powder and sugar.
2. Chop 2 rosemary sprigs; sprinkle over lamb. Keep remainder to throw on coals while cooking. Pour marinade over lamb. Cover and refrigerate about 3 hours. Bring lamb to room temperature.
3. Light a charcoal fire in an outdoor grill. Position grill 6 inches above coals. Remove lamb from marinade, reserving marinade. Pat lamb dry with paper towels. Season with pepper. When coals are evenly hot, place lamb on grill. Toss remaining rosemary sprigs on coals. Grill, turning often, until cooked to desired doneness, about 10 to 12 minutes. Baste meat with marinade during cooking. Makes 6 servings.

About 165 mg sodium per serving.

Stifado

5 tablespoons all-purpose flour
2 lbs. beef for stew, cut into 1-inch cubes
5 tablespoons vegetable oil
1/2 teaspoon cumin seeds
1 (2-inch) piece cinnamon stick
2 tablespoons tomato paste
3 tablespoons wine vinegar
3 cups Unsalted Beef Stock, page 78, or 3 cups water
  and 1 tablespoon very low-salt beef bouillon
  granules
Freshly ground pepper
2 teaspoons dried leaf thyme
1 lb. pearl onions, peeled
1/4 lb. low-salt cheese, cut into cubes

To garnish:
Minced parsley

Left to right: Stifado, Goulash Soup

The combination of spices, herbs and beef gives this casserole a very special flavor. Serve with boiled new potatoes tossed with unsalted butter or margarine and chives.

1. Preheat oven to 325F (165C). Place flour in a plastic bag. Add meat; shake until coated.
2. Heat oil in a large skillet. Add floured beef in batches; sauté until browned on all sides. With a slotted spoon, place browned beef in a large casserole dish.
3. Add cumin, cinnamon stick and tomato paste to skillet. Stir in vinegar, stock, pepper and thyme. Bring to a boil.
4. Pour mixture over meat. Cover and cook in preheated oven until meat is almost tender, about 1 hour.
5. Add onions; cover. Cook until onions are tender, about 30 minutes.
6. Sprinkle with cheese. Bake, uncovered, until cheese begins to melt, about 5 minutes. Sprinkle with parsley. Makes 6 servings.

Variation
Substitute 2 medium rabbits that have been cut up for beef.

About 100 mg sodium per serving.

Dilled Veal

4 (4- to 6-oz.) veal cutlets
Freshly ground pepper
1/4 cup unsalted butter or margarine
1 medium onion, finely sliced
1 tablespoon chopped dill or 1 teaspoon dill weed
Juice from 1 lemon

To garnish:
Dill sprigs, if desired

1. Season veal with pepper. Melt butter or margarine in a large skillet over medium heat. Add veal; sauté until cooked, about 10 minutes, turning.
2. Place veal on a platter. Add onion and dill to skillet. Sauté until onion is limp and starts to brown. Add lemon juice to skillet. Return veal; heat through.
3. Garnish with dill, if desired. Makes 4 servings.

About 75 mg sodium per serving.

Goulash Soup

2 tablespoons vegetable oil
2 onions, finely chopped
1 garlic clove, crushed
3/4 lb. beef for stew, cut into 1/2-inch cubes
1 tablespoon Hungarian paprika
1 tablespoon caraway seeds
1 tablespoon tomato paste
2-1/2 cups Unsalted Beef Stock, page 78, or 2-1/2 cups water and 2-1/2 teaspoons very low-sodium beef bouillon granules
Freshly ground pepper
Hot-pepper sauce
1 large potato, peeled, finely diced
1 carrot, finely diced
1 tablespoon chopped parsley

To serve:
1/2 cup plain yogurt or dairy sour cream

This is a good wholesome soup. It's ideal for a chilly night or a weekend lunch. Serve with Onion & Parsley Loaf.

1. Heat oil in a large saucepan or Dutch oven over medium heat. Add onions and garlic; sauté until softened.
2. Increase heat to medium-high. Add meat in batches; sauté until browned on all sides, stirring. Reduce heat. Add paprika and caraway seeds.
3. Stir in tomato paste and stock. Season with pepper and hot-pepper sauce.
4. Cover and simmer until meat is tender, about 1 hour. Add potato and carrot. Simmer until vegetables are tender, 20 minutes. Stir in parsley.
5. Ladle into bowls; top each serving with a spoonful of yogurt or sour cream. Makes 4 servings.

About 100 mg sodium per serving.

Sautéed Veal Cutlets

4 (4- to 5-oz.) veal cutlets
1 recipe Simple Marinade, page 78
1 cup fresh reduced-sodium-bread crumbs
2 tablespoons unsalted butter or margarine
3 tablespoons vegetable oil

1. Place cutlets in a shallow dish. Pour marinade over cutlets; cover and marinate 1 to 2 hours.
2. Remove with tongs. Dip into bread crumbs to coat.
3. Heat butter and oil in a large skillet. Add coated cutlets; sauté until browned and cooked through, about 10 minutes, turning once. Makes 4 servings.

Variation
Substitute 4 boned, skinned chicken-breast halves for veal. Pound chicken to 1/4-inch thick. Finish as directed above.

About 90 mg sodium per serving.

Seasonings for Goulash

Paprika gives goulash its distinctive and authentic flavor. Paprika can also be added to sauces for poached chicken or fish, hard-cooked eggs or cheese dishes.

Caraway seeds are also an important ingredient in goulash. The Germans and Austrians are passionate about them, using them in cakes, bread, sauerkraut and cheese dishes. Try adding them to potato or beet salad and to cooked red cabbage.

Bobotie

5 tablespoons vegetable oil
2 medium onions, finely chopped
1 lb. lean ground beef
1 tablespoon Mild Curry Powder, page 75
1 teaspoon ground turmeric
2 tablespoons wine vinegar
1/2 cup Unsalted Beef Stock, page 78, or 1/2 cup
   water and 1/2 teaspoon very low-sodium
   beef-bouillon granules
2 tomatoes, peeled, chopped
1 large low-sodium bread slice soaked in 1/4 cup milk
1/4 cup chopped almonds
1/2 cup raisins
1 tablespoon brown sugar
1 tablespoon apricot jam
2 eggs
1 cup milk
6 thin lemon slices
3 to 4 bay leaves

Bobotie is a traditional South African dish. It is to South Africa what moussaka is to Greece. Serve with rice and a tossed green salad.

Left to right: Bobotie; Liver Albanian Style, page 64; Groundnut Stew, page 41

1. Heat oil in a large skillet over medium heat. Add onions; sauté until golden. Add meat; sauté until just beginning to brown, stirring to break up meat.
2. In a small bowl, combine curry powder, turmeric and vinegar; stir into browned meat. Add stock and tomatoes; cook, uncovered, 15 minutes.
3. Preheat oven to 350F (175C). Lightly grease a shallow 2-quart baking dish. Squeeze milk from bread. Break bread into small pieces. Stir bread, almonds, raisins, brown sugar and jam into meat mixture.
4. Spoon mixture into greased baking dish. Bake in preheated oven 30 minutes.
5. In a medium bowl, beat eggs with milk. Strain over meat. Arrange lemon slices and bay leaves in egg mixture. Bake until custard is set, about 30 minutes. Remove bay leaves before serving. Makes 6 servings.

Variation
Substitute ground lamb for ground beef.

About 110 mg sodium per serving.

Braised Beef

1 (4-lb.) beef chuck roast
1 recipe Cooked Wine Marinade, page 78
2 tablespoons vegetable oil
3 tablespoons unsalted butter or margarine
2 onions, quartered
3 carrots, cut into 2-inch pieces
1 parsnip, cut into 1-inch pieces
2 celery stalks, cut into 1-inch pieces
Freshly ground pepper
3 tablespoons all-purpose flour blended with 3
  tablespoons unsalted butter or margarine
2 to 3 tablespoons red-currant jelly

To garnish:
Chopped parsley

Traditionally, braising is browning meat in hot fat, then cooking it slowly, in a covered casserole, with vegetables and a little liquid. This allows the flavors of the marinade and vegetables to permeate throughout the meat, as opposed to roasting which is cooking with radiant heat in an oven or on a spit over an open flame.

1. Place roast in a medium stainless steel or glass bowl. Pour marinade over roast. Cover and refrigerate up to 3 days. Lift out roast, reserving marinade. Pat roast dry with paper towels. Strain marinade; set aside.
2. Heat oil and butter or margarine in a Dutch oven. Add roast; sauté until browned on all sides, turning. Remove excess fat from pan.
3. Reduce heat. Add reserved marinade. Cover and simmer about 1-1/2 hours. Add vegetables; cook 1 hour or until meat and vegetables are tender.
4. Place roast on a platter. Remove vegetables with a slotted spoon; place in a serving bowl. Add flour-and-butter mixture to cooking liquid, a little at a time. Cook, whisking, until sauce thickens slightly.
5. Add red-currant jelly. Cook until smooth. Cut meat into slices. Spoon sauce over meat. Sprinkle with parsley. Serve vegetables separately. Makes 8 servings.

About 135 mg sodium per serving.

Carpet-Bag Steaks

4 beef loin tenderloin steaks, 1-1/2-inches thick
8 shucked oysters
Freshly ground pepper
1/4 cup unsalted butter or margarine
2 tablespoons vegetable oil
Juice of 1/2 lemon
2 tablespoons chopped fresh parsley

This recipe from Australia is an inspired combination of some of the best ingredients cooked in a simple yet delicious way.

1. Using a sharp knife, cut a 2-inch slit into side of each steak. Carefully extend cut about three-fourths of way through steaks. Gently make opening large enough for oysters. Place 2 oysters in each steak.
2. Grind lots of pepper on outside of each steak; pat down firmly.
3. In a large skillet, heat 2 tablespoons butter or margarine and oil over medium-high heat. Add steaks; sauté, turning often. Cook a total of 7 to 8 minutes for rare or 10 to 11 minutes for medium. Transfer to a hot serving dish.
4. Add remaining butter or margarine to skillet; add parsley and lemon juice. Pour over meat. Makes 4 servings.

About 150 mg sodium per serving.

Left to right: Frikadeller, Veal Goulash with Herb Dumplings

Chinese-Style Liver with Sage

2 medium carrots, sliced
3/4 lb. calves' liver
3 tablespoons cornstarch
3 tablespoons vegetable oil
1 teaspoon low-sodium soy sauce
1 tablespoon Chinese rice wine or sherry
1 tablespoon fresh sage leaves or 1 teaspoon rubbed
   sage
1/4 cup water
Freshly ground pepper
2 teaspoons sesame oil

---

1. Blanch carrots in boiling water in a medium saucepan 4 minutes. Drain; set aside.
2. Drain liver; pat dry with paper towels. Cut liver into 1/2-inch strips. Place cornstarch in a plastic bag. Add liver strips; toss to coat.
3. Heat vegetable oil in a large skillet or wok. Add coated liver; stir-fry until browned. Reduce heat. Cook 2 to 3 minutes. Remove with a slotted spoon; keep hot.
4. Add soy sauce, rice wine or sherry, sage and water to juices in pan. Cook until slightly reduced, stirring frequently.
5. Return liver to skillet or wok; add carrots and sesame oil. Cook until hot, stirring. Makes 4 servings.

About 75 mg sodium per serving.

Liver Albanian Style

1 medium onion, thinly sliced
1/2 teaspoon red (cayenne) pepper
3 tablespoons finely chopped parsley
1/2 teaspoon sugar
1 lb. calves' liver, cut into 1/2-inch-wide strips
1/4 cup Pernod or other anise-flavored liqueur
1 tablespoons all-purpose flour
3 tablespoons olive oil
1 red bell pepper, cut into rings or strips

Serve with aromatic Basmati rice.

1. In a small bowl, combine onion, cayenne, parsley and sugar; set aside.
2. In a medium bowl, combine liver and liqueur; let stand 15 minutes. Drain; pat dry on paper towels.
3. Toss liver in flour. Heat oil in a large skillet over medium-high heat. Add liver in batches; sauté until just beginning to brown and still slightly pink in center, 2 to 3 minutes. Drain on paper towels.
4. Arrange cooked liver on a serving dish. Garnish with onion mixture and bell pepper. Makes 4 servings.

About 90 mg sodium per serving.

Veal Goulash
with Herb Dumplings

3 tablespoons all-purpose flour
1-1/2 lbs. veal for stew, cut into 1-inch cubes
3 to 4 tablespoons vegetable oil
3 large onions, finely chopped
1 garlic clove, crushed
2 tablespoons Hungarian paprika
1 tablespoon tomato paste
2 cups Unsalted Beef Stock, page 78, or 2 cups water
    and 2 teaspoons very low-sodium beef-bouillon
    granules
1 teaspoon caraway seeds
1/2 cup dairy sour cream

Herb Dumplings:
10 low-sodium-bread slices
1 cup milk, warmed
1 tablespoon vegetable oil
1 medium onion, chopped
2 eggs, beaten
1/4 teaspoon white pepper
1/8 teaspoon ground nutmeg
1 teaspoon grated lemon peel
2 to 3 tablespoons chopped fresh mixed herbs, such as
    tarragon, parsley, thyme and marjoram

To garnish:
1/4 green bell pepper, cut into strips
1/4 red bell pepper, cut into strips

1. Preheat oven to 325F (165C). Place flour in a plastic bag. Add meat; toss to coat. Heat oil in a large skillet; add meat in batches; sauté until browned on all sides. Using a slotted spoon, transfer to a casserole dish.
2. Add onions and garlic to remaining oil; sauté until softened. Stir in paprika, tomato paste, stock and caraway seeds. Pour over meat. Cover and cook in preheated oven until meat is tender, 1-1/2 to 1-3/4 hours.
3. Meanwhile to make dumplings, break bread into small pieces. Place bread in a medium bowl; pour milk over bread. Heat oil in a medium skillet. Add onion; sauté until softened. Add sautéed onions, eggs, white pepper, nutmeg, lemon peel and herbs to bread mixture. Shape into about 16 small balls. Remove casserole from oven. Add dumplings. Cover and bake until dumplings are light and fluffy, about 20 minutes.
5. To serve, arrange dumplings around edge of a heated serving dish. Stir sour cream into goulash. Ladle into center of dumplings. Garnish with bell-pepper strips. Makes 6 servings.

About 140 mg sodium per serving.

Frikadeller

1 lb. ground veal
1 small onion, finely chopped
1/2 cup fresh low-sodium-bread crumbs
1 tablespoon chopped fresh parsley
Freshly ground pepper
A little freshly grated nutmeg
1 egg, beaten
About 1/2 cup all-purpose flour
Vegetable oil

Lemon & Tarragon Sauce:
6 tablespoons unsalted butter or margarine
1 garlic clove, crushed
1-1/2 tablespoons all-purpose flour
2/3 cup Unsalted Chicken Stock, page 79, or 2/3 cup
    water and 2/3 teaspoon low-sodium chicken
    bouillon granules
1 to 2 tablespoons sugar
Grated peel and juice of 1 large lemon
1 tablespoon chopped fresh tarragon or 1 teaspoon
    dried leaf tarragon
Dash hot-pepper sauce

These little meatballs can also be served with other sauces, as appetizers or as the main dish.

1. In a medium bowl, combine veal, onion, bread crumbs, parsley, pepper and nutmeg. Stir in as much egg as necessary to make a soft but non-sticky mixture.
2. Wet your hands with water. With your wet hands, shape mixture into about 24 walnut-size balls. Roll in flour to coat.
3. Heat oil in a large skillet. Add meatballs in batches; sauté until browned on all sides, about 8 minutes. Keep warm while preparing sauce.
4. To make sauce, melt butter or margarine in a medium saucepan. Add garlic; cook until softened. Stir in flour; cook 2 minutes, stirring constantly.
5. Slowly stir in stock. Cook until sauce begins to thicken, stirring.
6. Add sugar, lemon peel, lemon juice, tarragon and hot-pepper sauce. Stir until sugar dissolves. To serve, pour sauce into a serving dish. Arrange meatballs in another serving dish. Makes 4 servings.

Variation
Substitute lean ground beef for veal.

About 125 mg sodium per serving.

Side Dishes & Breads

Rice with Vegetables

3/4 cup long-grain white rice
1-1/2 cups water
Freshly ground black pepper
1/2 teaspoon dried leaf thyme
1 tablespoon unsalted butter or margarine
1 small onion, sliced
1 cup chopped broccoli
3 or 4 radishes, sliced
1/2 green or red bell pepper, diced
1 celery stalk, thinly sliced
1 cup canned unsalted whole-kernel corn, drained

1. To prepare rice, bring water to boil in a medium saucepan. Add rice, black pepper, thyme and butter or margarine; stir until combined. Bring to a boil.
2. Reduce heat. Cover and simmer until rice is tender and liquid is absorbed, 15 to 20 minutes.
3. Stir vegetables into hot rice. Cover and let stand 10 minutes before serving. Makes 4 servings.

Variation
Rice Salad: Cool vegetables and rice slightly. Spoon into a medium bowl. Toss with a vinaigrette dressing. Cover and refrigerate until chilled.

About 15 mg sodium per serving.

Saffron Rice Pilaf

A pinch of saffron threads
2 cups hot water
1 cup long-grain white rice
1/3 cup golden raisins
1 carrot, cut in julienne strips
1 tablespoon unsalted butter or margarine
1/2 medium onion, finely chopped
1 cup toasted slivered almonds

The raisins and carrot give a hint of sweetness to this dish.

1. In a medium saucepan, soak saffron in water about 10 minutes. Bring to a boil. Add rice, raisins, carrot, butter or margarine and onion; stir until combined. Bring to a boil.
2. Reduce heat. Cover and simmer until rice is tender and liquid is absorbed, 15 to 20 minutes.
3. Stir almonds into hot rice. Makes 4 servings.

About 20 mg sodium per serving.

Orange Rice

2-1/2 cups water
1 tablespoon grated orange peel
1/2 cup orange juice
Dash of hot-pepper sauce
2 tablespoons unsalted butter or margarine
1-1/2 cups long-grain white rice
1 orange, peeled, sectioned, if desired

1. Combine water, orange peel and orange juice, hot-pepper sauce, butter or margarine in a medium saucepan. Bring to a boil. Stir in rice. Bring to a boil.
2. Reduce heat. Cover and simmer until rice is tender and liquid is absorbed, 15 to 20 minutes. Let stand 5 minutes. Stir in orange sections, if desired. Makes about 4 cups or 6 to 8 servings.

About 5 mg sodium per serving.

Bulgur

3 tablespoons unsalted butter or margarine
1/2 cup pine nuts
4 green onions, sliced
2 cups bulgur
4 cups Unsalted Chicken Stock, page 79, or 4 cups
    water and 4 teaspoons low-sodium chicken-bouillon
    granules
Freshly ground pepper
2 teaspoons grated lemon peel
1/2 cup raisins

Bulgur, made from wheat, is eaten in the Middle East.

1. Melt butter or margarine in a medium saucepan. Add pine nuts; sauté until toasted. Stir in onions and bulgur. Add chicken stock and pepper. Bring to a boil.
2. Reduce heat. Cover and cook until liquid is absorbed and bulgur is soft, about 15 minutes. Stir in lemon peel and raisins. Makes 4 to 6 servings.

About 25 mg sodium per serving.

Clockwise from left: Bulgur, Saffron Rice Pilaf, Rice with Vegetables

Pita Bread

1 (1/4-oz.) pkg. active dry yeast (about 1 tablespoon)
1 teaspoon sugar
1-1/2 cups warm water (110F, 45C)
1/2 teaspoon salt
2 tablespoons vegetable oil
About 4-3/4 cups bread flour
Cornmeal

---

1. In large bowl of mixer, dissolve yeast and sugar in warm water. Let stand until foamy, 5 to 10 minutes.
2. Add salt, oil and 2-1/2 cups flour; beat until smooth, about 3 minutes. Stir in enough remaining flour to make a soft dough.
3. On a lightly floured surface, knead dough until smooth and elastic, 8 to 10 minutes.
4. Roll dough between your hands to make a 12-inch rope. Cut into 12 equal pieces. Shape each piece into a ball, pinching dough at bottom to seal. Cover with a dry towel; let rest 10 minutes.
5. Roll each ball into a 6-inch circle. Place circles on a lightly floured surface. Cover with dry towels. Let rise in a warm place, free from drafts, until doubled in bulk, about 20 minutes.
6. Arrange 1 oven rack at the lowest position and the other in center of oven. Preheat oven to 500F (260C). Lightly sprinkle 2 large baking sheets with cornmeal. Carefully transfer 3 circles to each prepared baking sheet.
7. Set 1 baking sheet with bread aside. Place remaining baking sheet on the bottom rack of oven. Bake 3 to 4 minutes or until puffed. Place on upper rack. Put remaining baking sheet with bread on bottom rack. Bake pitas on top rack about 3 minutes or until browned. Place baked pitas on racks to cool, 3 minutes. Wrap in foil or place in plastic bags to soften. Repeat procedure with remaining pitas.
8. Makes 12 pita-bread rounds.

About 82 mg sodium per pita round.

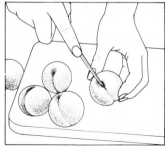

1/To peel peaches, make a small cut near stem end. Drop peaches into boiling water.

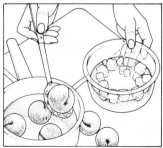

2/Remove peaches with a slotted spoon; place into ice water to cool quickly before peeling.

Eggplant Bake

1-3/4 lbs. eggplants
Freshly ground pepper
About 1 tablespoon vegetable oil

Tomato Sauce:
1 tablespoon olive oil
1 tablespoon unsalted butter or margarine
1 small onion, finely chopped
2 garlic cloves, crushed
1-1/2 lbs. tomatoes, peeled, coarsely chopped
Freshly ground pepper
1 teaspoon sugar
1 tablespoon each chopped parsley and basil
1 tablespoon tomato paste, if desired

Crumb Mixture:
1 cup fresh low-sodium-bread crumbs
2 tablespoons chopped fresh parsley
2 tablespoons chopped fresh basil

Blanching eggplant results in a less oily dish, which most people prefer. This dish can be served hot, warm or cold. Try it warm with yogurt for lunch or hot with roast lamb.

1. Cut eggplants into 1/2-inch slices. Plunge half into a large saucepan of boiling water; cook 3 minutes. Drain in a colander; pat dry with paper towels. Repeat with remaining eggplant.
2. To make tomato sauce, heat oil and butter or margarine in a medium saucepan. Add onion and garlic; sauté until softened. Add tomatoes, pepper, sugar and herbs. Reduce heat. Simmer, uncovered, until tomatoes are soft and sauce is beginning to thicken. Add tomato paste, if desired.
3. To make crumb mixture, in a small bowl, combine all ingredients; set aside.
4. Preheat oven to 350F (175C). Lightly grease a shallow casserole dish. Cover bottom of greased dish with 1/2 of eggplant slices. Cover with 1/2 of tomato sauce. Sprinkle with 1/2 of crumb mixture. Season with pepper. Repeat layers with remaining ingredients. Drizzle with oil.
5. Bake in preheated oven until eggplant is tender and mixture is bubbly, about 45 minutes. Makes 8 servings.

About 10 mg sodium per serving.

Spiced Peaches

3-1/2 cups sugar
1-1/2 cups malt vinegar
12 whole cloves
24 allspice berries
1 (1/2-inch) piece gingerroot
1 (2-inch) cinnamon stick
2-1/4 lbs. peaches (about 9 medium), peeled, see
   opposite
1 orange, sliced

1. Place sugar and vinegar in a large saucepan over medium heat; stir until sugar dissolves.
2. Place cloves, allspice, gingerroot and cinnamon into a cheesecloth bag; tie securely. Drop bag into pan.
3. Add peaches to syrup; bring to a boil. Reduce heat. Simmer until peaches are just tender, about 8 minutes. Spoon peaches into a large glass jar.
4. Cook orange slices in syrup 3 to 4 minutes; arrange in jar with peaches. Remove spice bag. Increase heat. Boil syrup until slightly reduced, 3 to 4 minutes.
5. Pour reduced syrup over peaches. Seal; cool to room temperature. Refrigerate at least a month. Serve with roast pork or duck. Makes about 2 quarts.

About 15 mg sodium per recipe.

Left to right: Eggplant Bake; Turkish-Style Stuffed Lamb, page 59

Sesame Loaf

1 cup milk
1/3 cup unsalted butter or margarine, room
   temperature
1 (1/4-oz.) pkg. active dry yeast (about 1 tablespoon)
1/4 cup sugar
3/4 cup warm water (110F, 45C)
1/2 teaspoon salt
About 5 cups bread flour
1 egg, beaten
1 tablespoon milk
1/4 cup sesame seeds, if desired

1. In a small saucepan over low heat, heat milk and butter
or margarine, stirring, until butter or margarine melts.
Cool to room temperature.
2. In a large bowl, dissolve yeast and 1 teaspoon sugar in
warm water. Let stand 5 to 10 minutes or until foamy.
3. Stir cooled milk mixture, remaining sugar and salt into
yeast mixture until blended. Add 3-1/2 cups flour; stir
until combined. Stir in enough remaining flour to make a
soft dough that comes away from side of bowl.
4. On a lightly floured surface, knead in enough remaining flour to make a stiff dough. Knead 8 to 10 minutes or
until smooth and elastic.
5. Clean and grease bowl. Place dough in greased bowl,
turning to coat all sides. Cover with a slightly damp towel.
Let rise in a warm place, free from drafts, until doubled in
bulk, about 45 to 60 minutes.
6. Grease a baking sheet. Punch down dough; divide into
2 pieces, making 1 piece 2/3 of dough. Shape large dough
piece into a slightly flattened ball; place on greased baking sheet. Shape small dough piece into a ball; place on
top of large piece of dough. Seal edge. Cover with a dry
towel; let rise until doubled in bulk. In a small bowl, beat
egg with milk. Brush egg mixture over dough. Sprinkle
with sesame seeds, if desired.
7. Preheat oven to 400F (205C).
8. Bake in preheated oven 40 to 45 minutes or until bread
sounds hollow when tapped on bottom. Remove from
baking sheet; cool completely on a wire rack. Makes 1
large loaf or 8 to 10 servings.

About 142 mg sodium per serving.

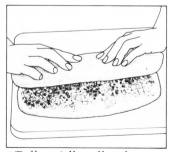 

1/Roll up jelly-roll style.
Seal seams.
     2/Cut into 8 equal pieces.

Onion & Parsley Loaf

1 (1/4-oz.) pkg. active dry yeast (about 1 tablespoon)
2 teaspoons sugar
1/2 cup warm water (110F, 45C)
1-1/2 cups bread flour
1-1/2 cups whole-wheat flour
1/2 teaspoon salt
1 teaspoon finely grated lemon peel
1 tablespoon unsalted butter or margarine
1/2 cup milk
Filling:
3 tablespoons unsalted butter or margarine
1 large onion, finely chopped
2 tablespoons chopped parsley
2 tablespoons chopped basil, oregano or marjoram
Freshly ground pepper

*This is a perfect party loaf. Each person can easily pull off
a portion. It teams well with soups for a family lunch or
supper.*

1. In a measuring cup, dissolve yeast and sugar in warm
water. Let stand until foamy, 5 to 10 minutes.
2. In a food processor fitted with the steel blade, combine
flours, salt, lemon peel and butter or margarine. Add yeast
mixture and milk; process until combined. Process 20
seconds to knead.
3. Grease a medium bowl, place dough in greased bowl,
turning to coat all sides. Cover with a slightly damp towel.
Let rise in a warm, draft-free, place until doubled in bulk,
about 30 minutes.
4. Meanwhile to make filling, melt butter or margarine in a
medium skillet. Add onion; sauté until softened, about 5
minutes. Stir in herbs. Let cool to room temperature.
5. Grease a 9-inch cake pan. Punch down dough. On a
lightly floured surface, roll out dough to a 14" x 8" rect-
angle.
6. Scatter cooked onion and herbs over dough, leaving a
1/2-inch edge. Sprinkle with pepper. Brush edge with
water. Roll up, jelly-roll style, starting from 1 long edge.
Seal seams. Cut into 8 equal pieces; place into greased
pan, cut-side down.
7. Let rise until doubled in bulk, about 15 minutes. Meanwhile, preheat oven to 375F (190C).
8. Bake in preheated oven until golden brown, 30 to 35
minutes. Turn out on a wire rack. Serve warm or cool.
Makes 8 servings.

About 135 mg sodium per serving.

Cucumber-Yogurt Salad

1 cucumber
1 small onion, finely chopped
1/2 cup plain yogurt
2 teaspoons chopped mint
2 teaspoons chopped parsley
Dash hot-pepper sauce

This is delicious with grilled lamb or pork.

1. Peel cucumber; remove seeds. Coarsely grate cucumber. Press moisture out of cucumber.
2. In a medium bowl, combine grated cucumber, onion, yogurt, mint, parsley and hot-pepper sauce. Cover and refrigerate 1 hour. Makes about 2 cups or 4 servings.

About 25 mg sodium per serving.

Left to right: Onion & Parsley Loaf; Canadian Chowder, page 18

Zucchini Pie

1 lb. zucchini, cut into 1-inch chunks
1/4 cup unsalted butter or margarine
1 small onion, chopped
1 garlic clove, crushed
4 medium tomatoes, peeled, chopped
1 teaspoon sugar
2 tablespoons chopped fresh herbs, such as parsley,
  chives and basil
4 eggs, beaten
1/2 cup shredded reduced-sodium Swiss cheese (2 oz.)
Freshly ground pepper

This dish is particularly versatile and can be served for a hot lunch or supper. Or cool and take on a picnic; cut into wedges. A little diced cooked potato or cooked rice can be added to the mixture, but do not add too much or the pie will be too firm.

1. Brush a 9-inch pie pan with oil. Cut a waxed-paper circle to fit bottom of pan. Line pan bottom with paper. This is important if dish is to be turned out and served cold.
2. Place zucchini and 1 tablespoon water in a medium saucepan over medium heat; cook until wilted. Add 2 tablespoons butter or margarine. Reduce heat. Cover and simmer until crisp-tender, about 5 minutes. Do not overcook. Using a slotted spoon, place zucchini into a medium bowl; set aside.
3. Melt remaining 2 tablespoons butter or margarine in a medium skillet. Add onion and garlic; sauté until softened. Reduce heat. Add tomatoes and sugar; simmer 5 minutes. Add 1 tablespoon herbs. Cook, uncovered, until tomatoes are soft and mixture is beginning to thicken, 10 to 15 minutes.
4. Preheat oven to 375F (190C). Add tomato mixture to zucchini. Cool slightly; stir in eggs, cheese, remaining 1 tablespoon herbs and pepper. Spoon into prepared pan.
5. Bake in preheated oven until firm to the touch, 20 to 25 minutes. Serve hot or at room temperature. Makes 4 to 6 servings.

About 115 mg sodium per serving.

Fennel Soup

1-1/4 lbs. fish bones, rinsed
5 cups water
1 onion, sliced
1 carrot, sliced
1 celery stalk, sliced
2 or 3 parsley sprigs
1 lb. fennel bulbs with tops
1 bay leaf
Fresh ground pepper
2 lemons
3 egg yolks
1 teaspoon Pernod, if desired

1. Place fish bones in a Dutch oven; cover with water. Add onion, carrot, celery and parsley sprigs.
2. Cut feathery leaves from top of fennel; reserve for garnish. Cut fennel bulb into quarters. Add fennel quarters.
3. Bring to a boil, skimming as necessary. Reduce heat. Add bay leaf and pepper. Cover and simmer until vegetables are tender, about 30 minutes.
4. Strain stock from vegetables and bones into a clean pan. Discard vegetables and bones. Cook until liquid is reduced to about 2-1/2 cups.
5. Cut 4 slices from lemons; reserve for garnish. Squeeze juice from remaining lemons. In a small bowl, combine lemon juice and egg yolks. Stir in 1/2 cup hot, not boiling, stock.
6. Stir stock mixture into remaining stock in pan; heat through. Do not boil.
7. Stir in Pernod, if desired. Ladle into bowls; top with a lemon slice and reserved fennel leaves. Makes 4 servings.

About 100 mg sodium per serving.

Dhal

1 cup split peas, soaked in water overnight, or lentils
1-1/2 cups water
2 medium onions, finely chopped
2 garlic cloves, crushed
1 (1/2-inch) piece gingerroot, finely chopped, or 1/2
  teaspoon ground ginger.
1 teaspoon ground turmeric
2 tablespoons vegetable oil
2 teaspoons Garam Masala, page 76
2 tablespoons unsalted butter or margarine

To garnish:
Cilantro leaves

This is a wonderful opportunity to use your homemade garam masala. The dhal is delicious served hot or warm. It's even better if made a day ahead and reheated before serving.

1. Place split peas or lentils in a medium saucepan; cover with water. Add 1 onion, 1 garlic clove, gingerroot or ginger and turmeric. Bring to a boil. Reduce heat. Cover and simmer until tender, 1 hour.
2. Heat oil in a medium skillet. Add remaining onion and garlic; sauté until golden. Add garam masala; cook 1 minute, stirring.
3. Stir sautéed ingredients into cooked lentils or split peas. Turn off heat; let stand about 15 minutes to blend flavors.
4. Add butter or margarine. Reheat until hot, stirring occasionally.
5. Garnish with cilantro leaves. Makes 4 servings.

About 25 mg sodium per serving.

Greek-Style Vegetables

1/2 cauliflower (about 1 lb.)
1 cup water
1 cup dry white wine
1/4 cup vegetable oil
1 teaspoon peppercorns, crushed
1 teaspoon coriander seeds
1/2 teaspoon fennel seeds
2 to 3 bay leaves
1 sprig each of thyme, parsley, marjoram or oregano
1 red bell pepper, cut into strips
1 green bell pepper, cut into strips
1/2 lb. leeks

To garnish:
Finely chopped fresh herbs

1. Break cauliflower into cauliflowerets; set aside.
2. Wash leeks thoroughly under running water; diagonally cut each leek into 3 or 4 pieces.
3. In a medium saucepan, heat water, wine and oil. Tie peppercorns, coriander, fennel, bay leaves, thyme, parsley and marjoram or oregano in a piece of cheesecloth to form a bag; add to saucepan. Bring to a boil.
4. Add cauliflowerets; cook, uncovered, until crisp-tender, 6 to 8 minutes. Remove with a slotted spoon; spoon into a medium heatproof bowl.
5. Add bell peppers to pan; cook, uncovered, 2 to 3 minutes only. Remove with a slotted spoon; add to cauliflowerets.
6. Finally, add leeks to pan; cook, uncovered, until softened, about 5 minutes. Pour leeks and liquid over other vegetables. Cool to room temperature. Cover and refrigerate several hours.
7. Bring to room temperature before serving. Discard cheesecloth bag. Spoon vegetables and a little of liquid into 4 individual dishes. Sprinkle with fresh herbs. Makes 4 servings.

About 20 mg sodium per serving.

Ratatouille

1/2 cup olive oil or other vegetable oil
1 garlic clove, crushed
2 medium onions, sliced
2 eggplants, about 1 lb. total, cut into 1/4-inch-thick slices
3/4 lb. zucchini, cut into 1/4-inch-thick slices
1 green bell pepper, cut into strips
1 red bell pepper, cut into strips
3 large tomatoes, peeled, cut into large wedges
1 tablespoon chopped oregano
1 tablespoon chopped basil
1 tablespoon chopped parsley
Freshly ground black pepper

This Mediterranean vegetable stew can be eaten either hot, warm or at room temperature. Serve as a starter or as a side dish with roasted or broiled meats.

1. In a large saucepan or Dutch oven, heat oil. Add garlic and onions; sauté until soft and transparent.
2. Add eggplant, zucchini and bell peppers to pan. Stir to coat all vegetables with oil. Reduce heat. Cover and cook 15 minutes, stirring occasionally.
3. Add tomatoes, oregano, basil, parsley and pepper. Cover and cook until vegetables are tender but retain their shapes, 10 to 15 minutes. Makes 4 servings.

About 15 mg sodium per serving.

Ratatouille

Mild Curry Powder

2 tablespoons whole cloves
2 tablespoons peppercorns
2 tablespoons cumin seeds
1 (2-inch) cinnamon stick
2 tablespoons cardamom pods
3 or 4 bay leaves
1/2 nutmeg, freshly grated (about 2 teaspoons)

1. Preheat oven to 350F (175C). Place cloves, peppercorns, cumin, cinnamon stick, cardamom pods and bay leaves on an ungreased baking pan. Bake in preheated oven until spices give off an aroma, about 5 minutes.
2. Cool spices. Break cinnamon into pieces; remove cardamom seeds from their pods. Blend or grind all spices together into a powder.
3. Add nutmeg. Store in an airtight container. Makes about 1/2 cup.

Less than 5 mg sodium per tablespoon.

Hot Curry Powder

2 teaspoons whole cloves
40 cardamom pods
1 (3-inch) cinnamon stick
4 teaspoons cumin seeds
3 tablespoons coriander seeds
1 teaspoon fenugreek seeds
1 teaspoon peppercorns
1 tablespoon chili powder or dried whole chilies
1/2 nutmeg, grated (about 2 teaspoons)
1 tablespoon ground turmeric

These quantities are a guide for the first time you make curry powder. You may decide that you prefer more or less of some ingredients. Don't make large quantities, because once ground, flavors will deteriorate. For longer storage, place in a small airtight container; keep in the freezer.

1. Preheat oven to 350F (175C). Place cloves, cardamom and cinnamon stick in an ungreased baking pan. Bake in preheated oven 10 minutes.
2. Meanwhile, in a heavy skillet over medium heat, heat cumin, coriander, fenugreek and peppercorns until spices give off an aroma, about 2 minutes, stirring constantly. Do not burn spices.
3. Cool spices. Break cinnamon stick into pieces; remove cardamom seeds from their pods. Blend or grind all spices together into a powder.
4. Add nutmeg and turmeric. Store in an airtight container. Makes about 1/3 cup.

Less than 5 mg sodium per tablespoon.

1. Fresh chili peppers, 2. Dried chili peppers, 3. Ground chili pepper, 4. Paprika, 5. Black peppercorns, 6. Cardamom pods, 7. Cardamon seeds, 8. Cinnamon sticks, 9. Fenugreek, 10. Tumeric, 11. Whole nutmegs, 12. Cumin seeds, 13. Coriander seeds, 14. Whole cloves

Coconut Milk

2-3/4 cups shredded coconut (about 8 oz.)
2 cups boiling water

1. In a blender or food processor fitted with the steel blade, process coconut and water 20 seconds.
2. Strain mixture through a sieve into a large bowl. Press mixture in sieve with a wooden spoon to extract as much liquid as possible.
3. Use immediately or freeze for future use. If desired, freeze in ice-cubes trays, then pack in plastic freezer bags. Makes about 2 cups coconut milk.

About 38 mg sodium per recipe.

Garam Masala

1/4 cup cumin seeds
2 tablespoons peppercorns
24 cardamom pods
2 teaspoons whole cloves
1 (3-inch) cinnamon stick

1. Preheat oven to 350 (175C). Spread all ingredients in a baking pan. Bake in preheated oven 5 minutes, turning occasionally.
2. Cool spices. Break cinnamon into pieces; remove cardamon seeds from their pods. Blend or grind all spices together into a powder.
3. Store in an airtight container. Makes about 1/4 cup.

Less than 5 mg sodium per tablespoon.

Watercress Mayonnaise

1 bunch watercress, finely chopped
2 egg yolks
White pepper
1/4 teaspoon dry mustard
1 tablespoon white-wine vinegar
1 cup olive oil or vegetable oil

1. In a blender or food processor fitted with the steel blade, combine watercress, egg yolks, white pepper, mustard and vinegar. Process until pureed.
2. With motor running, add oil through feed tube in a slow, steady stream. Process until thick and creamy. Cover and refrigerate up to 1 week. Makes 2 cups.

About 36 mg sodium per recipe.

Marinades

A marinade is a mixture of ingredients, such as wine or lemon juice, herbs, spices and aromatic vegetables, in which meat, poultry and fish are soaked for a time before cooking. The wine and lemon juice act as a tenderizer as well as flavoring agents. Oil is sometimes added to marinades that are also used for basting during cooking.

For centuries, a marinade was the accepted way to tenderize meat. Now the emphasis in more on the flavor added from the many herbs and spices in the marinade.

Mustard & Dill Mayonnaise

2 tablespoons Dijon-style mustard
2 teaspoons dry mustard
1 tablespoon sugar
2 tablespoons herb-flavored vinegar
1/2 cup olive or other vegetable oil
3 tablespoons chopped fresh dill or 1-1/2 tablespoons
   dill weed

It is worth searching for fresh dill, because it makes a big difference in flavor. Keep dill stems, refrigerated, in water with a plastic bag over the top. This is a way to keep herbs fresh for days. If using dill weed, make mayonnaise ahead so flavors have time to blend. Store leftover mayonnaise in the refrigerator. Whisk before serving. This mayonnaise is delicious with fish salads.

1. In a small deep bowl, combine Dijon-style mustard, dry mustard, sugar and vinegar.
2. Whisking constantly, add oil in a slow, steady stream. Whisk until thick. Whisk in dill. Cover and refrigerate up to 1 week. Makes about 1 cup.

About 370 mg sodium per recipe.

Mayonnaise

2 egg yolks
1/4 teaspoon white pepper
1/2 teaspoon dry mustard
1 tablespoon lemon juice or white-wine vinegar
1-1/4 cups olive oil or other vegetable oil or a
   combination

1. In a food processor fitted with the steel blade, combine egg yolks, white pepper, mustard and lemon juice or vinegar. Do not overprocess.
2. With motor running, add oil through feed tube in a slow, steady stream. Use immediately, or cover and refrigerate up to 1 week. Makes about 1-1/2 cups.

Variation
Finely chopped herbs can be added to finished mayonnaise.

About 36 mg sodium per recipe.

Lemon Butter

1/2 cup unsalted butter or margarine, room
   temperature
Grated peel and juice of 1/2 lemon

Use Maitre d'Hotel, Tarragon or Watercress Butters for fish, chicken or veal. Use Garlic Butter for steaks and Chive or Mint Butters for lamb and pork.

1. In a small bowl, beat butter or margarine until fluffy. Beat in lemon peel and lemon juice until combined.
2. Cut an 8-inch foil square. Spoon butter mixture into center of square; form butter mixture into a roll. Refrigerate until firm before sealing. When firm, wrap foil around butter mixture. Seal ends. Label and refrigerate or freeze. Slices can then be cut from roll as required. Makes about 1/2 cup.

Variations
Maitre d'Hotel Butter: Beat 2 tablespoons finely chopped parsley into Lemon Butter.
Garlic Butter: Stir 2 finely chopped garlic cloves into Maitre d'Hotel Butter.
Tarragon Butter: Beat 2 tablespoons finely chopped tarragon into Lemon Butter.
Chive Butter: Omit lemon peel and lemon juice. Beat 1 teaspoon grated onion and 1 to 2 tablespoons chopped chives into Lemon Butter.
Mint Butter: Blanch 1/4 cup packed mint leaves in boiling water 30 seconds. Drain; pat dry on paper towels. Finely chop. Beat into Lemon Butter.
Watercress Butter: Prepare as for Mint Butter, using leaves from 1 bunch of watercress.

About 1 mg sodium per tablespoon.

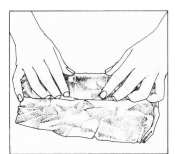

1/Roll foil tightly around chilled butter mixture, forming a roll.

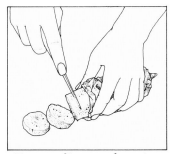

2/To use, slices can be cut as needed.

Unsalted Beef Stock

1 lb. beef for stew, cut into 1-inch pieces
2 lbs. beef soup bones
1 lb. veal bones
1 large onion, quartered
1 medium carrot, coarsely chopped
2 celery stalks, coarsely chopped
3 whole cloves
1 bay leaf
1 teaspoon peppercorns
3 parsley sprigs
3 or 4 thyme sprigs or 1 teaspoon dried leaf thyme
1 cup dry red wine

1. Preheat oven to 375F (190C). Place meat and bones in a roasting pan. Roast in preheated oven until lightly browned, 30 to 40 minutes, stirring 2 or 3 times.
2. Add onion, carrot and celery; cook until vegetables start to brown, 30 minutes. Place browned meat, bones and vegetables in a large Dutch oven or soup pot.
3. Skim fat from pan dripping. Over high heat, stir 1 cup water into pan to deglaze, scraping up browned bits. Add to browned meat mixture.
4. Add enough water to cover meat mixture by about 3 inches. Bring to a boil. Skim off foam as necessary. Boil until no more foam forms.
5. Reduce heat. Add cloves, bay leaf, peppercorns, parsley, thyme and wine. Cover and simmer at least 4 hours, adding water as necessary to keep ingredients covered.
6. Strain stock, pressing down on meat and vegetables. Discard meat, bones, vegetables and seasoning.
7. Cool stock by pouring into a large container and placing in a sink of cold water. Cool to room temperature. Pour into smaller containers; cover and refrigerate until chilled. Remove congealed fat.
8. Refrigerate up to 3 days or freeze up to 3 months. Makes about 3 quarts stock.

About 50 mg sodium per cup.

Simple Marinade

1 egg, beaten
2 teaspoons finely grated lemon peel
1 teaspoon lemon juice
1 teaspoon finely chopped tarragon or parsley
1 tablespoon vegetable oil
Freshly ground pepper

Use this marinade for fish, veal or poultry.

1. In a small bowl, combine egg, lemon peel and lemon juice, tarragon or parsley, oil and pepper.
2. Use immediately. Makes enough marinade for 2 pounds fish, chicken or veal.

About 70 mg sodium per recipe.

Cooked Wine Marinade

3 to 4 tablespoons vegetable oil
1 onion, chopped
T carrot, sliced
2 celery stalks, chopped
2 or 3 garlic cloves, crushed
2 cups red or dry white wine
1/2 cup wine vinegar
1 tablespoon juniper berries, crushed
1 tablespoon coriander seeds, crushed, or 1
   tablespoon ground coriander
1 teaspoon peppercorns, crushed
3 bay leaves
2 sprigs each of rosemary, thyme and parsley

Use this marinade for beef, lamb, pork or game.

1. Heat oil in a medium saucepan. Add onion, carrot, celery and garlic; sauté until lightly browned.
2. Add wine and vinegar, juniper berries, coriander, peppercorns, bay leaves, rosemary, thyme and parsley. Bring to a boil. Reduce heat. Simmer, uncovered, 20 minutes.
3. Cool to room temperature. Pour cooled marinate over lamb, pork or beef. Cover and refrigerate up to 3 days, basting twice a day. Marinate game up to 2 days. After marinating, roast or braise meat as directed in recipe. Makes enough marinade for a large roast.

About 85 mg sodium per recipe.

Master Marinade for Chicken

1 small onion, finely chopped
1 garlic clove, crushed
Juice of 1 small lemon
1 cup dry white wine
1 tablespoon chopped fresh herbs, such as tarragon,
    thyme or oregano, or 1 teaspoon dried leaf herbs
Freshly ground pepper

1. In a small bowl, combine all ingredients.
2. Marinade can be made ahead. Pour into a container with a tight fitting lid. Refrigerate up to 2 days. Makes enough marinade for 1 chicken.

About 18 mg sodium per recipe.

Unsalted Chicken Stock

2 lbs. chicken parts
1 medium onion, chopped
1 medium carrot, chopped
6 leafy celery tops
3 or 4 parsley sprigs
3 or 4 thyme sprigs or 1 teaspoon dried leaf thyme
1 bay leaf
1 teaspoon peppercorns

This recipe can be doubled. Freezing stock in ice cube trays is a convenient way to always have stock on hand.

1. Place chicken in a Dutch oven; add water to cover chicken by about 3 inches. Bring to a boil. Skim off foam as necessary. Boil until no more foam forms.
2. Reduce heat. Add onion, carrot, celery, parsley, thyme, bay leaf and peppercorns. Cover and simmer about 2 hours, adding additional water as necessary to keep chicken and vegetables covered.
3. Strain stock, pressing down on chicken and vegetables. Discard chicken, vegetables and seasoning.
4. Cool stock by pouring into a large container and placing in a sink of cold water. Cool to room temperature. Pour into smaller containers; cover and refrigerate until chilled. Remove congealed fat.
5. Refrigerate up to 3 days or freeze up to 3 months. Makes about 1-1/2 quarts stock.

About 30 mg sodium per cup.

Fennel Soup, page 72

Index